Introduction

1. Book Presentation and Objectives
2. Why AI is crucial for business in the 21st century
3. Current Landscape of AI in Business
4. Challenges and opportunities of implementing AI in the business environment
5. How to Use This Book: Reading Guide

Part I: Fundamentals of Artificial Intelligence in Business

Chapter 1: Understanding Artificial Intelligence

1. Definition of AI and its basic components
2. Main types of AI: Machine learning, neural networks, natural language processing (NLP)
3. Weak AI vs Strong AI: Outlook and Future
4. Ethics and AI: Ethical Considerations and Regulations

Chapter 2: Impact of AI on Business

1. Sectors and business areas most impacted by AI
2. Competitive advantages of AI adoption
3. Case studies of companies that have successfully integrated AI

4. Risks of not adopting AI in an environment of accelerated competition

Chapter 3: The Life Cycle of AI Projects

1. Phases of development and implementation of AI projects
2. Introduction to AI Data Models and Algorithms
3. Data preparation and management for AI projects
4. Evaluation and continuous improvement of AI models

Part II: Practical Implementation of AI in Business

Chapter 4: Diagnosis and Evaluation of AI Maturity in a Company

1. How to assess the current level of AI adoption
2. Diagnostic tools for AI maturity
3. Identifying key areas for AI integration
4. Evaluation of available resources (talent, technology, budget)

Chapter 5: Strategies for Developing an AI Culture

1. Changing mindset towards technological innovation
2. AI Staff Training: Roles and Skills
3. Leadership strategies to foster AI adoption
4. Collaboration between IT teams and business areas

Chapter 6: Selecting AI Tools and Platforms

1. AI Platforms and Software Most Used in Business
2. Comparison between in-house development options vs commercial solutions
3. Guide to selecting AI and cloud computing providers
4. Deploying AI in the cloud vs on-premise

Chapter 7: Planning and Execution of AI Projects

1. Defining the objectives and scope of an AI project
2. Return on Investment (ROI) Calculation in AI
3. AI Project Management Strategies
4. Monitoring and success metrics for AI projects

Part III: Applications of AI in Key Business Functions

Chapter 8: AI in Marketing and Customer Experience

1. Personalizing the customer experience with AI
2. Predictive Analytics for Marketing
3. Ad campaign automation and targeting
4. Examples of chatbots and virtual assistants in customer service

Chapter 9: AI in Finance and Risk Analysis

1. AI models for financial forecasting
2. Risk assessment and mitigation using AI
3. Fraud detection and transaction monitoring
4. Investment optimization with AI

Chapter 10: AI in Human Resources and Talent Management

1. Recruitment and selection with AI: Automation and ethical bias
2. Performance Evaluation and Talent Development
3. Analysis of work environment and employee retention
4. Chatbots and assistants for staff support

Chapter 11: AI in Operations and Logistics

1. Supply chain optimization with AI
2. Application of AI in inventory management
3. Route optimization and transportation management
4. Examples of robotics and AI in manufacturing

Chapter 12: AI in Innovation and Product Development

1. Rapid prototyping and simulation using AI
2. AI for demand forecasting and product planning
3. AI-Aided Design Applications
4. Disruptive innovation with AI in new product development

Part IV: Challenges and Ethical Considerations in AI

Chapter 13: Data Management and Privacy in AI Projects

1. The importance of data quality and security
2. Privacy and data protection laws (GDPR, CCPA)
3. Privacy Principles by Design
4. Protocols for anonymization and management of sensitive data

Chapter 14: Ethics and Responsibility in the Use of AI

1. Biases in AI Models: Causes and Solutions
2. Transparency in algorithms and social responsibility
3. AI and the Future of Work: Effects on Employment
4. Ethical Framework for the Implementation of AI in Business

Part V: Practical Guide to Implementing AI Projects

Chapter 15: Step-by-Step Implementation Examples

1. Implementing a Customer Service Chatbot
2. Product recommendation model for e-commerce
3. Automating HR processes with AI
4. Implementing a Sales Prediction Model

Chapter 16: Practical Tools and Resources

1. List of Free and Paid Tools for AI
2. AI Training & Course Platforms for Enterprises
3. Open resources and communities to learn and collaborate on AI
4. Templates and guides for starting an AI project

Conclusion

1. **Summary of Benefits and Key Strategies**
2. **Future of AI in Business and Next Steps**
3. **Final Tips for Sustainable AI Adoption**

Annexes

- Glossary of technical terms
- Recommended bibliography
- Additional Case Studies
- Self-assessment checklist for the implementation of AI in a company
- Contact resources and AI communities

Prologue

Today, artificial intelligence (AI) has ceased to be a simple technological curiosity and has become an essential and transformative component in the business world. As organizations seek to stay competitive in an increasingly dynamic and digitized environment, the adoption of AI-based solutions is presented not only as a strategic advantage, but as a fundamental necessity. In this context, we are pleased to present this book, a comprehensive guide designed to provide an in-depth and practical understanding of artificial intelligence in the business environment.

This book is the result of a careful compilation of knowledge, experiences, and best practices in the use of AI in various industries. From marketing and customer service to human resource management and operations optimization, each chapter offers a comprehensive analysis of how AI is redefining the rules of the game and setting new frontiers in the way companies interact with their customers, optimize their processes, and create sustainable value.

As Hospitality Prime representatives, we understand the complexities and challenges that businesses face in the pursuit of innovation and continuous improvement. We've seen how effective AI implementation can revolutionize the way customer relationships are managed, operational processes are optimized, and data-driven strategic decisions are made. Through this book, we want to empower business leaders, managers, and professionals with the knowledge and tools needed to navigate this exciting world of opportunities offered by artificial intelligence.

In addition to addressing the practical applications of AI, this book also delves into the ethical and responsibility aspects that must be considered when implementing these technologies. The importance of addressing bias, data privacy, and impact on employment are core issues that cannot be ignored in our pursuit of a future where AI coexists with a human approach to business.

We hope that this book will not only serve as a guide for AI implementation, but also inspire business leaders to adopt an innovative mindset and explore new ways to harness the potential of artificial intelligence on their path to success. We invite you to dive into its pages, explore each chapter, and use the insights and strategies shared here to transform your vision and operations in the digital age.

Welcome to this exciting journey into the future of business.

Hospitality Prime

Introduction

- **Book Presentation and Objectives**

This book is designed to be a comprehensive and accessible guide that demystifies artificial intelligence and demonstrates its real value in the business world. In an era where data is considered "the new oil" and technological innovations follow one another at breakneck speed, artificial intelligence (AI) has gone from being a futuristic concept to an essential tool in modern business. Through its pages, we seek to provide a deep and accessible understanding of AI, breaking down its fundamentals and exploring how it can be integrated into various business areas to increase efficiency, improve decision-making, and ultimately generate competitive advantage.

The objectives of this book are several. First, we want to offer a comprehensive understanding of what AI actually entails in the business context, addressing everything from the basics to the most advanced applications. Second, we intend to guide the reader in the planning and implementation of AI projects in your organization, presenting practical tools, methodologies, and strategies to carry out effective adoption. Finally, we aim to inspire, demonstrating that AI is not just a fad or a technology reserved for tech giants; It is an accessible opportunity for businesses of all sizes and industries that want to thrive in an ever-changing environment.

- **Why AI is crucial for business in the 21st century**

Artificial intelligence is, without a doubt, one of the most important technological developments of the 21st century. In a world where competitiveness has become increasingly fierce and change is constant, the ability to adapt and anticipate trends makes the difference between success and irrelevance. AI allows businesses to make informed decisions in real-time, analyze huge volumes of data to detect patterns that would otherwise go unnoticed, and improve efficiency in areas such as customer service, logistics, and production. This added value not only helps optimize operations, but allows companies to innovate in ways that were previously unimaginable.

AI is revolutionizing industries as varied as healthcare, banking, retail, and manufacturing, providing solutions to problems that were previously considered unsolvable. From predicting market trends to personalizing the customer shopping experience, artificial intelligence offers a range of possibilities that not only streamline processes, but also open doors to new business models. For many companies, AI adoption is no longer optional; It is a necessity to stay relevant and competitive in a globalized and digital market. This book explores how companies can embrace AI to not only improve their current operations, but also to redefine their market position and build the future of their industries.

- **Current Landscape of AI in Business**

Artificial intelligence is no longer a distant promise and has become a tangible reality in the business world. Large and small companies are adopting AI to solve specific problems and optimize their processes. For example, in the retail sector, AI makes it possible to predict customer behavior and personalize the offer based on their preferences, increasing conversion rates. In banking and finance, AI is used to detect fraud, analyze risks, and automate repetitive tasks. In the manufacturing sector, smart robotics is transforming the way goods are produced, improving both efficiency and accuracy.

Despite its growing adoption, the implementation of AI is not without its challenges. Many companies lack the data infrastructure and technical talent needed to develop and maintain effective AI systems. There are also concerns about data privacy and potential biases in algorithms, which can affect the fairness and transparency of their decisions. However, as technology continues to evolve and businesses become more familiar with its capabilities, AI adoption continues to increase. In this book, we'll explore how businesses can overcome these challenges and harness the potential of AI in every area of their operations.

- **Challenges and opportunities of implementing AI in the business environment**

Implementing artificial intelligence in an enterprise environment can bring with it a number of challenges, especially for those organizations that are unfamiliar with the technology or lack the necessary resources for its development and maintenance. One of the main obstacles is data infrastructure: for AI to be effective, companies must have clean, organized, and accessible data. In addition, the implementation of AI requires specialized technical skills, including knowledge in data science, programming, and handling advanced algorithms, which involves significant hiring or training effort. Another major challenge is the initial cost, as developing and deploying AI systems often requires a considerable investment.

However, the long-term benefits of AI far outweigh these initial challenges. AI not only improves operational efficiency, but also offers new ways to interact with customers, optimize the supply chain, and develop innovative products. Companies that successfully implement AI have the opportunity to improve decision-making, reduce costs, and find new revenue streams. This book will address each of these challenges and opportunities, providing strategies and tools for companies to effectively implement AI and make the most of its potential.

- **How to Use This Book: Reading Guide**

This book is structured to be a practical and accessible guide, designed both for those who have a basic understanding of artificial intelligence and for those who want to deepen their implementation and applicability in the business world. The first part of the book provides an introduction to the fundamentals of AI, including essential technical concepts and their impact on the business world. In this section, readers will be able to familiarize themselves with the key terms and tools that are the basis of AI, understanding how they work and how relevant they are.

In the following sections, the book discusses strategies for diagnosing a company's AI maturity level and how to develop an organizational culture that facilitates its adoption. Chapters dedicated to practical implementation are designed to guide the reader through each step of an AI project, from planning to execution to monitoring results. Case studies and practical examples are also presented to help visualize the process in a real context. Finally, the book explores the applications of AI in various business areas, addressing the associated ethical and technical challenges and presenting a practical guide to tools and resources.

The reader can choose to follow the book from beginning to end or focus on chapters that address specific topics of interest. For those who are already familiar with the basics of AI, the implementation and practical applications sections will be especially useful. The goal is for this book to be a go-to tool for both business leaders and technical professionals, providing them with the knowledge needed to strategically and sustainably integrate AI into their organizations.

Part I: Fundamentals of Artificial Intelligence in Business.

Chapter 1: Understanding Artificial Intelligence

In this first chapter, we will explore the conceptual basis of artificial intelligence (AI), breaking down its key components, types, and applications in the business context. Understanding the essence of AI is critical for anyone who wants to harness its benefits in business, as a clear view of its fundamentals allows for informed and realistic decisions to be made about its implementation. AI is not just a technology; It is a paradigm shift that is transforming the way companies approach problems, optimize processes, and design innovative solutions.

Definition of AI and its basic components

Artificial intelligence is defined as the ability of a machine to perform tasks that, if done by humans, would require intelligence. This includes activities such as speech recognition, language interpretation, decision-making, learning from data, and adapting to new environments. On a technical level, AI is made up of several subfields, each of which contributes to machines becoming "smart". These include machine learning, computer vision, natural language processing (NLP), expert systems, and more. Each of these subfields has its own set of algorithms and techniques, which work together to simulate different aspects of human intelligence.

Within the basic components of AI, **machine learning** plays a fundamental role, as it allows machines to improve their performance through experience. This is achieved by algorithms that identify patterns in large volumes of data and use them to make predictions or classifications. Another essential component is **computer vision**, which allows machines to interpret and understand images and videos, a crucial capability in applications such as surveillance, manufacturing, and autonomous vehicles. Natural **language processing** (NLP) allows machines to understand and generate human language, making it possible for people and machines to interact through spoken or written language. These combined components endow AI with flexibility and learning potential that make it especially powerful in the business environment, as it can be applied in a variety of areas to solve complex problems.

Main types of AI: Machine learning, neural networks, natural language processing (NLP)

The main types of AI used in business today are machine learning, neural networks, and natural language processing, each with unique capabilities and applications.

1. **Machine learning**: This type of AI focuses on teaching machines to learn from data.

Unlike traditional systems that follow pre-established rules, machine learning allows algorithms to identify patterns and improve over time, becoming an invaluable tool for predicting behaviors, automating decisions, and personalizing the customer experience. In the business context, machine learning is widely used to analyze customer data, forecast demand, and optimize inventories.

2. **Neural networks**: Inspired by the workings of the human brain, neural networks are a system of interconnected algorithms that allow machines to recognize complex patterns. Neural networks are the foundation of many modern advances in AI, especially in areas such as computer vision and speech recognition. Their ability to learn hierarchical representations of data makes them ideal for complex tasks, such as image classification and fraud detection in financial transactions.

3. **Natural Language Processing (NLP):** This field allows machines to understand, interpret, and generate human language in a natural way. Through NLP, companies can develop virtual assistants, customer service

chatbots, and sentiment analysis systems that process customer feedback in real time. This ability to understand language allows companies to improve customer relations, automate customer service, and analyze trends on social networks.

Each of these types of AI has its own set of techniques and applications that, when combined, create a powerful synergy. In the enterprise arena, the joint use of machine learning, neural networks, and NLP allows organizations to better adapt to market demands and deliver customized services that meet their customers' expectations.

Weak AI vs Strong AI: Outlook and Future

AI can be classified into two broad categories: **weak AI** and **strong AI**, each with different goals, capabilities, and applications. Weak AI, also known as narrow AI, refers to systems designed to perform specific tasks within a limited scope. Examples of weak AI include voice assistants such as Siri or Alexa, which can answer questions or execute commands, but do not possess a general understanding of all human knowledge. Weak AI is the predominant technology today and is the one that is transforming companies in terms of operational efficiency, process automation and personalization of services.

On the other hand, **strong AI**, also called artificial general intelligence (AGI), refers to systems that can understand, learn, and apply knowledge in a similar way to human intelligence. Unlike weak AI, strong AI would have a reasoning and adaptive capacity comparable to that of a person, allowing it to perform on a wide variety of tasks without specific limitations. Although strong AI is still theoretical, its development raises both promise and concerns for the future. In the business arena, strong AI could revolutionize the landscape, allowing machines to make complex strategic decisions and play leadership roles.

The evolution towards strong AI poses significant challenges, especially in the ethical and regulatory field, as well as questions about the interaction between humans and machines in a work environment. Meanwhile, weak AI continues to be the driving force behind today's innovations and represents the starting point for companies to integrate AI into their operations.

Ethics and AI: Ethical Considerations and Regulations

The implementation of AI in business is not without ethical and regulatory issues. AI, like any other powerful technology, has the potential to be used for both good and evil, and it is the responsibility of companies and governments to ensure that its use is beneficial and fair to society. One of the main ethical challenges of AI is the **possible generation of biases** in its algorithms. Since AI systems learn from data, any bias present in that data can lead to outcomes that discriminate against certain groups or individuals, thus creating inequalities in areas such as employment, financial services, and healthcare.

In addition, AI raises **concerns about data privacy**. AI systems often collect and analyze large volumes of personal data in order to make informed decisions, making it necessary to implement privacy and data protection policies to prevent the misuse of personal information. Regulations such as the General Data Protection Regulation (GDPR) in Europe and the California Consumer Privacy Act (CCPA) in the United States seek to protect the privacy of individuals by imposing strict rules on how companies can collect and use data. In this book, we'll explore how businesses can comply with these regulations and build AI systems that respect user privacy.

Finally, **accountability and transparency** in AI decision-making are essential to avoid ethical issues and ensure trust in AI systems. Today, many AI algorithms operate as a "black box," meaning that their decision-making processes are not always understandable or replicable. This can lead to situations where decisions are made without a clear justification, affecting customers, employees, and other actors. Throughout this book, not only are the technical aspects of AI addressed, but the importance of developing ethical policies and practices for use in the business environment is also emphasized.

Chapter 2: Impact of AI on Business

Artificial intelligence is transforming the way businesses operate, creating new opportunities to optimize processes, deliver personalized products and services, and compete more effectively in a global marketplace. This chapter takes an in-depth look at the impact of AI on business, exploring the sectors and business areas where AI has left a particularly significant footprint, the competitive advantages of its adoption, examples of success in companies across various sectors, and the risks faced by those that choose not to adopt it. Understanding these aspects allows business leaders to make informed decisions about how to strategically integrate AI into their organizations.

Sectors and business areas most impacted by AI

AI is affecting almost all sectors of the economy in a transversal way, but there are some where its impact has been particularly profound and transformative. In the **retail** sector, for example, AI is used to analyze purchasing patterns, forecast product demand, and personalize the customer experience. AI algorithms allow retailers to anticipate consumer needs and offer personalized recommendations, increasing conversion rates and customer loyalty. In addition, AI systems optimize the supply chain, reducing costs and improving delivery times.

The **financial sector** is another big beneficiary. AI makes it possible to analyse large volumes of data in real time to detect fraud, predict risks and personalise financial products. In banking, AI algorithms process transactions to identify suspicious activity, while in the investment market, AI is used to spot trends and make quick and accurate decisions. The ability to predict financial behavior allows companies to better manage their portfolios and create products tailored to their customers' needs.

In **the healthcare sector**, AI is revolutionizing the way diseases are diagnosed and treatments are developed. AI allows doctors to analyze medical images with impressive accuracy, helping to detect diseases at early stages and propose personalized treatments. Precision medicine and medical decision support systems are just some of the applications of AI in this sector. In addition, AI algorithms help in hospital management, optimizing resource allocation and improving operational efficiency.

The **manufacturing industry** is another area where AI has had a significant impact. In smart factories, AI enables the automation of repetitive tasks, real-time quality monitoring, and predictive maintenance of machinery, reducing downtime and operating costs. Through AI, manufacturers can predict machine failures before they occur, thereby maximizing efficiency and improving productivity. The optimization of production processes not only reduces costs, but also allows companies to respond quickly to fluctuations in demand.

The list of sectors impacted by AI continues to grow and includes areas such as **marketing**, where AI is used to segment audiences and personalize messages, and **human resources**, where AI helps in the selection and evaluation of candidates. These examples illustrate how AI is transforming entire industries, providing companies with new tools to improve their competitiveness and adapt to market changes.

Competitive advantages of AI adoption

AI represents a competitive advantage on multiple levels, and companies that adopt it can differentiate themselves from their competitors in significant ways. One of the key advantages is operational **efficiency**. AI makes it possible to automate repetitive processes, freeing employees from monotonous tasks and allowing them to focus on higher-value strategic activities. This not only reduces operating costs, but also improves the accuracy and speed of processes, increasing the overall efficiency of the company.

Another competitive advantage of AI is its ability to **improve the customer experience**. Thanks to AI, companies can offer more personalized experiences, anticipate consumer needs, and respond to consumer queries quickly and effectively. AI systems such as chatbots, virtual assistants, and personalized recommendations allow businesses to interact with customers instantly and in real-time. Not only does this improve customer satisfaction, but it also increases retention and loyalty rates, which is key in saturated and highly competitive markets.

The **ability to analyze data in real-time** also gives businesses a strategic advantage. In an environment where data is a critical resource, AI makes it possible to process and analyze large volumes of information in real time, generating insights that allow companies to make informed decisions and act quickly in the face of changes in the market. AI allows companies to understand their customers' preferences, identify business opportunities, and continuously improve their products or services, resulting in a differentiated value proposition.

In addition, AI allows companies to **innovate in their business models**, creating new products and services that were not possible before. Companies that integrate AI can explore new lines of business, such as implementing services based on personalized subscriptions, developing intelligent products, and creating interactive experiences that enhance customer relationships. In this sense, AI not only represents an operational improvement, but also drives innovation, allowing companies to adapt to an ever-evolving market and stay ahead of the curve.

Case studies of companies that have successfully integrated AI

Over the years, many companies have demonstrated how AI adoption can lead to dramatic results in terms of efficiency, customer satisfaction, and innovation. One of the most well-known examples is Amazon, whose e-commerce platform uses AI to personalize product recommendations to each user based on their browsing and purchase history. Amazon's AI also optimizes logistics and inventory management, reducing costs and improving delivery times, which has been key to its overall success.

Another notable case is that of **Netflix**, which has revolutionized the entertainment industry through personalized content recommendation. Thanks to its AI algorithms, Netflix is able to analyze the preferences and consumption patterns of its users to suggest series and movies that interest them, increasing the time users spend on the platform and improving their user experience. This strategy not only increases subscriber retention, but also allows Netflix to optimize its content offering and make informed decisions about new productions.

In the field of health, **IBM Watson** has been a pioneer in the application of AI for medical research and diagnosis. Using natural language processing and deep learning, Watson can analyze large volumes of medical literature and clinical data to help clinicians identify accurate treatments and diagnoses. IBM Watson AI has proven its value in areas such as oncology, where it helps healthcare professionals identify personalized therapies for their patients, thereby improving clinical outcomes.

Finally, in the financial sector, **JPMorgan Chase** uses AI to analyze legal contracts at a much faster speed than humans, reducing the time it takes to review complex legal documents. This use of AI not only saves time, but also reduces the risk of errors in contract review, improving the accuracy and efficiency of your legal processes. These examples demonstrate how AI can be effectively integrated into various sectors, offering tangible benefits that drive competitiveness and innovation.

Risks of not adopting AI in an environment of accelerated competition

In a world where technology is advancing by leaps and bounds, not adopting AI can pose a significant risk to businesses. Those organizations that resist change face the danger of falling behind compared to their competitors who do take advantage of the advantages of AI. One of the most obvious risks is the **loss of efficiency**: in sectors where AI makes it possible to automate tasks and improve the accuracy of processes, companies that do not adopt this technology are forced to operate less efficiently, which can result in higher costs and lower productivity.

The **loss of competitiveness** is another fundamental risk. In saturated markets, the ability to innovate and differentiate is crucial to attracting and retaining customers. Companies that don't implement AI miss out on the opportunity to deliver personalized experiences, tailor their products and services to consumer preferences, and respond quickly to market changes. In an environment where consumers are increasingly demanding personalization and convenience, companies that do not adopt AI risk losing relevance and not being able to meet their customers' expectations.

In addition, the lack of AI adoption can lead to limited **analytical and decision-making capabilities**. AI allows companies to analyze large volumes of data in real time, generating valuable insights for strategic decision-making. Without AI, businesses rely on traditional methods of analysis, which are not only slower, but also limit the ability to adapt to emerging trends. In industries where agility and adaptability are key to survival, not having AI can be a critical disadvantage.

Finally, companies that do not adopt AI also face the risk of **missing out on innovation opportunities**. AI makes it possible to create new business models, develop intelligent products, and explore new lines of service. By not taking advantage of this technology, companies not only miss an opportunity to grow, but also expose themselves to being overtaken by more innovative competitors that have integrated AI into their strategies.

Chapter 3: The Life Cycle of AI Projects

The lifecycle of artificial intelligence (AI) projects is made up of several critical phases that must be carefully managed to ensure effective development and successful implementation. As companies adopt AI projects, it's vital that they understand each phase of the lifecycle to optimize their resources, reduce risk, and maximize impact. This chapter explores each of the stages, from data planning and preparation to the implementation and continuous improvement of AI models, providing comprehensive guidance for achieving robust and sustainable results over time.

Phases of development and implementation of AI projects

The development and implementation of AI projects can be divided into several phases, each with specific objectives and activities that allow work teams to structure and manage projects effectively.

1. **Defining the problem and project objectives**: In this initial phase, the team should clearly identify the problem that the AI project aims to solve, define specific objectives, and establish indicators of success. Accurate problem identification is critical as it will guide technical decisions and help align the project with the company's strategic goals.
2. **Exploration and selection of tools and technologies**: Once the problem is clearly defined, the next step is to select the AI tools, frameworks, and technologies that will be used to solve it. This decision will depend on factors such as the type of data, performance requirements, and technical capabilities of the equipment. Tools such as TensorFlow, PyTorch, and development environments such as Jupyter Notebook are common in AI development.
3. **Data collection and preparation**: Data collection is one of the most crucial tasks in AI projects, as the quality and quantity of data directly influence the effectiveness of

the model. This phase involves collecting, cleaning, and preprocessing the data that will feed the model, making sure that it is well-structured and free of noise or irrelevant information.
4. **Development and training of the model**: With the data prepared, the AI model is selected and trained. In this phase, algorithms are applied to the data and models are fine-tuned so that they learn to identify relevant patterns and relationships. The training process involves adjusting the model's parameters to optimize its performance on the training dataset, and it often requires multiple iterations and adjustments to achieve the desired level of accuracy and efficiency.
5. **Model evaluation and validation**: Model evaluation is critical to ensure that it functions properly and is able to generalize to new data. This is achieved by validating the model on a different dataset than the one used for training. Common indicators for evaluating performance include accuracy, sensitivity, specificity, and F1 score, among others.
6. **Deployment and deployment of the model**: Once the model has been evaluated and optimized, it is implemented in the production environment. At this stage, it's important to ensure that the model is accessible and scalable, and that it integrates

seamlessly into the company's existing systems. Implementation may involve configuring APIs, creating user interfaces, and adapting the model to the operational needs of the business.

7. **Continuous monitoring and improvement**: After deployment, it is essential to monitor the performance of the model and make continuous adjustments to maintain its accuracy and usefulness. AI models can deteriorate over time due to changes in data or market conditions, so continuous monitoring is critical to maintaining their effectiveness.

Introduction to AI Data Models and Algorithms

AI models are mathematical or statistical representations that are used to capture patterns in data and make predictions or classifications. The most common models in AI include regressions, decision trees, neural networks, and vector support machines, among others. The choice of model depends on the type of problem to be solved and the nature of the available data.

- **Regression and classification**: These models are ideal for problems in which you want to predict a numerical value or categorize data into different groups. Linear regression, for example, is used to predict continuous variables, such as future sales, while classification models, such as decision trees, are employed to categorize data, such as segmenting customers.
- **Neural networks and deep learning**: Neural networks are inspired by the workings of the human brain and are especially useful for complex problems involving large amounts of data, such as image processing and speech recognition. Deep learning, a branch of neural networks, uses multiple processing layers to break down and analyze complex patterns in unstructured data, being critical for advanced applications such as natural language processing and computer vision.

- **Vector support machines (SVMs):** This type of algorithm is effective for classification and regression problems where it is important to find the optimal margin separating different classes of data. SVMs are commonly used in text classification and image recognition applications.

Each AI model has its strengths and weaknesses, and the appropriate selection will depend on factors such as the type of data, the complexity of the problem, and accuracy requirements. This chapter explores these models in detail and provides guidelines for choosing the most suitable one for each business project.

Data preparation and management for AI projects

Data preparation is one of the most critical and laborious phases in the lifecycle of an AI project, as AI models can only be as good as the data on which they are trained. Data management in AI involves a number of activities ranging from data collection to data cleaning, transformation, and proper storage.

1. **Data collection**: Data quality is vital to the success of the AI model, and the collection phase should focus on obtaining relevant, representative, and sufficient data. The collection can come from internal sources, such as enterprise databases, or external sources, such as social networks, third-party APIs, or public data.
2. **Data cleansing**: Raw data often contains errors, duplicates, missing values, and other imperfections that can affect model performance. Data cleansing involves identifying and correcting these problems by removing duplicates, correcting errors, and handling null values. This process ensures that the data is accurate and consistent.
3. **Data transformation and normalization**: Data must be transformed into a format suitable for AI models, which involves converting categorical data into numerical data, standardizing scales, and applying techniques such as normalization or

standardization to prevent certain attributes from dominating others. Normalization ensures that the data is in a uniform range, improving the stability and accuracy of the model.
4. **Data management and storage**: Finally, data management includes organizing and storing data in a way that is accessible and secure. This may involve the use of database management systems or big data platforms, which allow large volumes of data to be stored and made easy to access in the later phases of the project.

Data preparation and management is critical not only to train models, but also to ensure that they can be correctly generalized to new data, improving their ability to make accurate predictions in real-world situations.

Evaluation and continuous improvement of AI models

The evaluation and continuous improvement phase is key to ensuring that AI models maintain their effectiveness over time. AI models can see their performance decrease due to changes in data, changing behavior patterns, or new external factors, making constant monitoring and regular adjustments essential.

1. **Model evaluation**: Evaluating models involves analyzing their performance using specific metrics that vary depending on the type of problem and the model used. Common metrics include accuracy, recall, area under the ROC curve, and mean squared error. The evaluation allows you to identify possible errors or limitations of the model and verify if it meets the objectives of the project.
2. **Cross-validation and testing on multiple datasets**: To prevent the model from over-conforming to training data and misgeneralizing to new data, cross-validation is used. This method divides the data into multiple subsets, training and evaluating the model in different combinations to ensure that performance is consistent across various scenarios.
3. **Continuous monitoring and recalibration**: Once the model is deployed, continuous

monitoring is essential to detect potential drops in performance. This process involves tracking key metrics in real-time and making recalibration adjustments when necessary, especially if the data environment changes over time.

4. **Continuous improvement and model adjustments**: Continuous improvement refers to the process of optimizing the model over time. This may involve retraining it with new data, adjusting hyperparameters, or in some cases, completely changing the model if new, more efficient techniques or algorithms emerge. This phase is crucial to ensure that the model maintains its accuracy and relevance over time, maximizing its value to the business.

Through these phases of evaluation and continuous improvement, AI projects can adapt to changes and continue to generate value over time, ensuring that AI investments produce consistent and sustainable results.

Part II: Practical Implementation of AI in Business

The practical implementation of artificial intelligence in business is a process that demands careful strategic planning and a realistic assessment of the current situation of the company. To integrate AI effectively, it is essential to know the state of readiness of the organization and determine the areas where it can generate the most value. This section explores the path to practical AI adoption, providing detailed guidance for conducting diagnostics, setting clear goals, and organizing the resources needed to successfully undertake AI projects.

Chapter 4: Diagnosis and Evaluation of AI Maturity in a Company

The implementation of artificial intelligence in business is not simply about incorporating state-of-the-art technology; It requires the company to be prepared in terms of culture, talent, infrastructure, and strategy. Before starting any AI project, it is essential to carry out a detailed diagnosis to assess the maturity of the company with respect to the adoption of this technology. Understanding the current level of AI maturity helps identify strengths and areas of opportunity where investment is needed to ensure effective and sustained integration. This chapter focuses on how companies can conduct a comprehensive assessment, from analyzing the current level of AI adoption to assessing the resources and capabilities required to implement it.

How to assess the current level of AI adoption

Assessing a company's current level of AI adoption is the first step in understanding how mature it is with the technology. This diagnosis involves analyzing what AI tools and techniques are already in use, how they are being used, and what the real impact is on business operations and outcomes. Some companies may be at a nascent stage, where they are just beginning to explore AI in pilot areas, while others may have moved towards deeper integration, using machine learning algorithms to improve key processes or make strategic decisions.

The adoption diagnosis also includes assessing the **understanding and acceptance of AI** in organizational culture. This involves looking at the extent to which employees and managers understand the benefits of AI and see it as a strategic tool and not simply a technological change. Companies with an innovation-oriented culture and continuous learning mindset are typically more prepared to adopt AI effectively, while those with rigid structures and resistance to change may face significant challenges in its implementation. In this diagnosis, it is critical to conduct interviews with the different departments and gather feedback on how they perceive AI, as these opinions can indicate whether there is a positive disposition or cultural barriers that could hinder the success of AI in the business.

Another important part of this assessment is the **analysis of current processes that could benefit from AI.** Here it is about identifying areas where AI can bring significant improvements, such as supply chain optimization, personalization of the customer experience or automation of repetitive administrative tasks. Reviewing current processes and their level of automation and digitalization allows us to understand which of them are susceptible to being enhanced by AI algorithms. Through this assessment, a clearer view of the current state of AI adoption in the enterprise and the specific opportunities for applying the technology is obtained.

Diagnostic tools for AI maturity

There are a variety of diagnostic tools and frameworks that help companies assess their AI maturity level in a structured and detailed way. These tools offer clear methodologies and criteria to measure a company's readiness and ability to adopt AI in different areas. One of the most widely used methodologies is the **AI Maturity Model**, which classifies organizations into various stages of AI maturity, from initial exploration to comprehensive transformation, in which AI is a central component of the business strategy.

A robust diagnostic framework typically looks at several key factors, such as **organizational culture, technology infrastructure, data availability, AI talent,** and **strategic leadership**. Each of these factors is evaluated on a scale of development, from basic to advanced level, allowing the company to understand in which areas it is well positioned and in which it needs improvement. For example, if a company has an advanced technological infrastructure but lacks specialized AI talent, the diagnosis will indicate the need to invest in hiring or training personnel in areas such as machine learning or data analysis.

Assessment tools such as the **Digital Maturity Index (DMI)** and the **Data Science Maturity Model** are also useful for measuring the company's capacity in terms of data analysis and digitization, which are essential for the development of AI projects. These tools typically include surveys, interviews, and questionnaires designed to gather detailed information about the company's current capabilities and its leaders' level of engagement with AI. In addition, some tools offer comparisons of the company's position against others in its sector, which allows you to understand if it is aligned with industry trends or if it needs to make adjustments to catch up with its competitors.

Identifying key areas for AI integration

Once the company's maturity level has been assessed, the next step is to identify key areas where AI can generate tangible and relevant value. In many companies, priority areas often include **customer service**, **logistics and supply chain**, **sales optimization,** and **human resource management**, as these are functions where AI can bring significant improvements in efficiency and quality.

For example, in **customer service**, AI can help personalize the experience, provide real-time recommendations, and improve response times through chatbots and virtual assistants. These tools allow you to automatically respond to the most common queries, while human agents can focus on solving more complex problems. By integrating AI into customer service, companies not only improve consumer satisfaction, but also optimize their human resources, which is especially valuable in companies in sectors such as retail or e-commerce, where speed and accuracy in response are critical factors.

In the case of **logistics and supply chain**, AI can be used to forecast product demand, optimize distribution routes, and anticipate inventory issues. AI algorithms can analyze large volumes of sales, seasonality, and market trend data to make predictions that allow the company to prepare its inventories more effectively. In this way, storage costs are reduced and problems of shortages or excess inventory, which negatively affect profitability, are avoided.

Another area where AI can make a big difference is in **human resources**. AI can streamline recruitment processes, identify candidates with specific skills, and evaluate employee performance using talent analysis tools. AI systems allow HR departments to select the best candidates based on a broad set of criteria, making it easier to hire the right talent for the company's strategic needs.

Identifying key areas for AI allows companies to allocate their resources optimally and prioritize the most impactful projects. By concentrating on strategic areas, AI not only improves operational efficiency, but also drives innovation and enables the company to respond more nimbly and effectively to changes in the market.

Evaluation of available resources (talent, technology, budget)

Implementing AI in a company requires a careful assessment of the resources needed, both human and technical and financial. This assessment allows the company to determine if it has the right talent, the necessary technological infrastructure and sufficient budget to undertake AI projects in a sustainable way.

One of the first factors to evaluate is **human talent**. AI projects typically require a team of specialists in areas such as data science, machine learning, data engineering, and software development. In addition, it is important that the team includes business profiles capable of translating business requirements into technical AI objectives. If the company does not have the necessary internal talent, it may consider options such as hiring external staff, collaborating with universities or research centers, or training current employees in AI skills. The latter option can be especially beneficial, as it helps create an AI culture within the company and ensures a deeper understanding of projects by the team.

Technology **and infrastructure** are equally crucial to AI development. This includes everything from data storage and processing systems to the availability of development platforms and AI tools. AI projects often require large amounts of data and powerful processing capabilities, so the company should evaluate whether it has the right servers and storage systems in place, or whether it needs to invest in cloud platforms that allow it to access flexible and scalable processing resources. The technology also includes AI software, such as development frameworks and data visualization tools, that make the work of data scientists easier and speed up the development process.

Finally, **budget evaluation** is essential to ensure the viability of AI projects. Implementing AI in a company involves an initial investment in technology, talent, and training, as well as a recurring budget for the maintenance and improvement of models over time. In addition to investing in technology and talent, it is important to anticipate the costs of adapting processes and training employees. An adequate budget ensures that AI projects can run smoothly and that the company is prepared to meet financial challenges that may arise along the way.

The evaluation of these resources helps the company to have a realistic vision of its ability to adopt AI and allows for strategic planning of the necessary investments, optimizing the cost-benefit ratio and ensuring a sustainable approach over time. By ensuring that resources are aligned with project objectives, the company can move forward with AI adoption with confidence, minimizing risks and maximizing its return on investment.

Chapter 5: Strategies for Developing an AI Culture

The adoption of artificial intelligence in a company goes far beyond implementing advanced technology; it requires a profound cultural transformation. In an AI-oriented organization, each member understands and supports the benefits of this technology, and the company actively fosters a mindset of innovation and adaptability. To achieve this change, it is necessary to work on multiple levels: transform the mindset towards technological innovation, train staff in the necessary skills, establish committed leadership and foster interdepartmental collaboration. This chapter explores in depth how to develop an AI culture that is inclusive, progressive, and aligned with the company's strategic goals.

Changing mindset towards technological innovation

Changing mindsets is the first step in creating an AI culture in the company. For many organizations, AI represents a sea change in the way they operate, and this transformation requires employees to overcome the perception that AI is just a fad or a threat to their jobs. Instead, AI should be seen as a tool that enhances the capabilities of the company and its workers, providing new opportunities and improving existing processes.

One of the main challenges in generating this change in mindset is **to overcome the natural resistance to change**. The adoption of AI can raise fears, especially in industries where there is an idea that automation could displace jobs. To address these fears, it is important to clearly communicate that AI does not seek to replace people, but to allow them to focus on tasks with greater added value and creativity, while technology takes care of repetitive or complex tasks from a computational point of view. This shift in perspective helps employees understand how AI can improve their daily work, motivating them to learn and supporting its adoption.

An effective strategy to facilitate this change is **to show concrete examples** of how AI can benefit the company and its employees. This can include success stories from other companies in the sector or internal pilots that demonstrate the tangible value of AI in areas such as time optimization, error reduction or improved customer experience. With these examples, employees can see the benefits of AI in action and understand that this technology offers real opportunities to improve their own tasks and outcomes.

AI Staff Training: Roles and Skills

To build a strong AI culture, it is critical to train staff in the skills needed to work in an AI-driven environment. As AI becomes a key component of business strategy, all employees should have a basic understanding of how it works, how it is applied in the business, and how they can interact with it in their day-to-day functions. In addition, it is essential to form a core of specialized talent that can lead AI projects and make the most of the technology's capabilities.

There are several key roles in the AI ecosystem that companies need to identify and foster within their teams. These roles include **data scientists**, **machine learning engineers**, **data analysts,** and **developers of specialized AI software**. Each of these profiles brings specific skills that are essential for the development and implementation of AI solutions in the company. Data scientists, for example, are responsible for analyzing large volumes of data and creating predictive models, while machine learning engineers focus on designing and improving the algorithms that allow AI to learn and adapt.

In addition to these technical roles, it's also crucial to train other employees on a more general level on AI. **AI literacy** for employees from different areas allows everyone to have a basic understanding of the concepts and capabilities of this technology, helping them identify how they could apply it in their work and how to interact with AI systems that can be implemented in the organization. Not only does this facilitate collaboration between technical and non-technical teams, but it also creates an environment where every employee is motivated to find opportunities for improvement through AI.

Training strategies can range from **introductory workshops and continuous learning programs** to partnerships with universities and training centers specializing in AI. Investing in AI training and skills development not only strengthens the company's technical capacity, but also promotes a learning environment that facilitates innovation and prepares the organization to face the technological challenges of the future.

Leadership strategies to foster AI adoption

Leadership plays a critical role in creating an AI culture within the company. For AI to be successfully adopted, organizational leaders must be the first to **embrace technology transformation** and clearly communicate the benefits and goals of AI. This type of technology-driven leadership allows the organization to see AI adoption not as a simple technology initiative, but as a strategic pillar for growth and innovation.

Effective AI leadership involves **establishing a clear vision** for how AI will benefit the company and its employees, promoting a culture of openness and collaboration. Leaders must be able to inspire their teams and show a genuine commitment to integrating AI into business processes. This vision must be constantly communicated through internal channels and in strategic meetings, allowing employees to understand the role of AI within business objectives and feel motivated to participate in this transformation.

Additionally, it's important for leaders to develop **incentive strategies** to encourage AI adoption. This can include everything from bonuses and recognition for those employees who are trained in AI, to reward programs for teams that lead innovative projects with this technology. It is also helpful for leaders to identify and support **AI champions** within the organization, i.e., employees who become internal role models in the use and promotion of AI. These champions can help spread AI culture at all levels of the company and motivate their peers to adopt a mindset of continuous innovation.

Finally, leaders must be committed to developing a **culture of trial and error** around AI. Experimentation is a critical component in AI development, and leaders should encourage teams to try new ideas and learn from failures. Fostering an environment where error is seen as a learning opportunity allows employees to feel more comfortable exploring the possibilities of AI and contributes to a culture of constant innovation.

Collaboration between IT teams and business areas

A successful implementation of AI in the enterprise requires close collaboration between IT teams and different business areas. AI should not be seen as just a technical initiative; It is a strategic tool that can directly impact the efficiency, productivity and competitiveness of the company. To maximize their value, AI projects must be aligned with business objectives and developed jointly between technical teams and operational areas.

This collaboration begins with **open and ongoing communication** between IT and business departments. Business leaders must be willing to share their goals and challenges, allowing IT teams to deeply understand the specific needs of each area. At the same time, IT teams need to be able to explain the capabilities and limitations of AI in a way that is accessible to business users, so that both parties can set realistic expectations and define practical solutions.

In many cases, building **multidisciplinary teams** for AI projects is an effective strategy to ensure collaboration between IT and business. These teams include not only technology experts, but also representatives of the business areas who have a deep understanding of the organization's processes and objectives. The combination of technical and business knowledge makes it possible to identify the best applications for AI and design solutions that truly meet operational needs. These teams can also act as benchmarks for other departments, facilitating the integration of AI across the enterprise.

Another key strategy is to implement a **co-creation approach**. As IT teams develop AI models, business users can provide continuous feedback on their functionality and applicability. This feedback allows the models to be adjusted and improved so that they really add value in the context of each area. In addition, business users can identify additional use cases for AI, helping to expand its deployment and leverage across the organization.

Collaboration between IT and business is essential to developing an AI culture that is both technical and strategic. This integration ensures that AI is not only implemented effectively, but also generates tangible benefits aligned with business objectives, allowing the company to achieve a significant competitive advantage in its sector.

Chapter 6: Selecting AI Tools and Platforms

The selection of AI tools and platforms is a crucial step in the successful implementation of AI projects in any organization. The wide variety of options available on the market can be overwhelming, but the right choice can make all the difference in the performance, scalability, and sustainability of AI solutions. This chapter discusses the different types of AI platforms and software most commonly used in business, as well as a comparison between in-house development options and business solutions. In addition, guidance is provided for selecting AI and cloud computing vendors, as well as a discussion on deploying AI in the cloud versus on-premise solutions.

AI Platforms and Software Most Used in Business

The most commonly used AI platforms and software in business are varied, and each offers specific features that can meet different business needs. Among the most prominent platforms are **Google Cloud AI, Microsoft Azure AI, IBM Watson,** and **Amazon Web Services (AWS).** Each of these platforms provides a diverse set of tools that allows companies to develop and deploy AI solutions tailored to their specific requirements.

Google Cloud AI is known for its data analytics capabilities and advanced machine learning tools. It offers solutions such as AutoML, which allows users with no coding experience to create custom AI models. On the other hand, **Microsoft Azure AI** stands out for its integration with other Microsoft tools and its wide range of cognitive services that facilitate natural language processing, image recognition and sentiment analysis tasks, which is particularly useful for companies that already use Microsoft products in their daily operations.

IBM Watson, for its part, has positioned itself as a leader in the field of enterprise artificial intelligence, offering robust solutions for data analysis and process automation. Its ability to understand natural language and its focus on deep learning make it a popular choice for businesses looking to implement advanced chatbots or customer service solutions. Finally, **Amazon Web Services (AWS)** stands out for its scalability and the variety of services it offers, from tools for machine learning to big data analytics capabilities, making it ideal for businesses looking for flexibility and expansion as they grow.

In addition to these platforms, there are also **specialized software solutions** that address specific needs. For example, tools such as **H2O.ai** and **DataRobot** allow users to build machine learning models without the need for deep technical knowledge, facilitating the democratization of AI within companies. In addition, **data visualization** tools such as Tableau and Power BI are essential for interpreting the results of AI models and enabling data-driven decision-making.

The choice of AI platform or software should align with the company's strategic goals, considering factors such as ease of use, scalability, integration with existing systems, and total cost of ownership. Each company needs to evaluate which of these solutions best suits its needs and technical capacity, seeking to maximize the return on investment in its AI projects.

Comparison between in-house development options vs commercial solutions

When companies decide to implement AI solutions, one of the most critical decisions they face is whether to develop the technology in-house or acquire commercial solutions already available in the market. Each approach has its advantages and disadvantages, and the right choice will depend on a variety of factors, including the business context, available resources, and long-term goals.

In-house **development** gives companies full control over the creation and customization of their AI solutions. This can be particularly beneficial for organizations that have very specific requirements or that operate in a niche market where business solutions may not be suitable. In addition, developing in-house allows the company to adapt the technology to its unique processes and evolve the solution as its needs change. However, this option is often more expensive and requires a significant investment in talent, infrastructure, and time. Companies must be prepared to face the technical challenges that come with software development and AI model management.

On the other hand, opting for **business solutions** presents its own set of benefits. These solutions are typically off-the-shelf, allowing for faster deployment and fewer risks associated with developing technology from scratch. Many trading platforms have been tested and optimized in a variety of business environments, meaning they can deliver reliable performance with less effort. In addition, technical support and updates are often included, freeing internal teams from the burden of maintaining and updating software.

However, business solutions may be less flexible and customizable than those developed in-house. If the solution is not a perfect fit for the specific needs of the business, compromises may need to be made in terms of functionality. Additionally, license and subscription fees can add up over time, making total cost of ownership harder to predict in the long run.

In conclusion, the decision between in-house development and commercial solutions should be a strategic assessment that considers the company's specific needs, technical capabilities, and budget. Many companies opt for a hybrid approach, where they develop custom solutions for critical areas while using business tools for more general functions.

Guide to selecting AI and cloud computing providers

Choosing AI and cloud computing providers is a crucial process that can determine the success or failure of a company's AI projects. When looking for a suitable vendor, organizations should consider several key criteria that impact the effectiveness, security, and scalability of proposed solutions.

First, it is critical to assess **the vendor's reputation and expertise** in the AI and cloud computing space. This includes researching their track record of implementation in similar companies, their success stories, and their ability to handle projects of different scales. Vendors with strong AI expertise typically offer not only advanced technology, but also insights and best practices that can help the company avoid common mistakes and optimize their implementation.

The **level of support and customer service** offered by the provider is also a crucial aspect to consider. A good vendor should provide ongoing technical support and assistance in integrating the technology into the company's existing processes. Responsiveness and quality of customer service can make a big difference in the implementation experience and troubleshooting issues that may arise later.

Security and compliance are other essential considerations, especially in a context where data is a valuable asset and its protection is critical. Companies must ensure that suppliers comply with relevant regulations and offer robust data protection and information security measures. Inquiring about security infrastructure, data encryption, and compliance certifications can provide greater peace of mind about protecting sensitive information.

Finally, it is important to evaluate **the scalability and flexibility of the solutions offered**. As the company grows, its technology needs will change as well. As such, it is vital to select a provider that offers scalable and flexible options, allowing the company to adapt the solution as it evolves. This can include the ability to integrate new functionality, adjust cloud resource usage, and perform updates efficiently.

In short, selecting AI and cloud computing providers is a process that requires careful research and evaluation of various criteria. Making informed decisions at this stage can facilitate a smoother and more successful implementation of AI initiatives in the enterprise.

Deploying AI in the cloud vs on-premise

The implementation of AI solutions can be carried out in two main ways: in the cloud or on on-premises servers. Each approach has advantages and disadvantages, and the choice between the two depends on the specific needs of the company, its resources, and its long-term strategy.

Deploying AI in the cloud has become a popular choice among many organizations due to its **scalability, flexibility, and cost reduction**. Cloud computing platforms allow businesses to access powerful computational resources without the need for large upfront investments in physical infrastructure. This means that businesses can scale their operations quickly, adding more processing and storage capacity as needed. In addition, cloud solutions often offer advanced AI tools and services that are regularly updated, ensuring that businesses have access to the latest technology and continuous improvements.

Another significant benefit of cloud deployment is the **ease of collaboration**. With cloud solutions, geographically distributed teams can access the same resources and data in real-time, making it easier to work together on AI projects. This ability to collaborate is especially important in an increasingly globalized business environment.

However, there are concerns related to the **security and privacy of data** in the cloud. For some companies, especially those that handle sensitive information or are subject to strict privacy regulations, the idea of storing data on external servers can be a hurdle. In these cases, organizations may choose to implement **on-premise** solutions, where servers and data are kept within the company's infrastructure, providing greater control over security and information management.

Implementing on-premise AI can also be beneficial for organizations that require **very low latencies** or that need to perform intensive real-time data processing, where immediate response time is critical. However, this option often comes with higher costs, both in terms of upfront investment in hardware and long-term maintenance and upgrade.

The choice between deploying AI in the cloud or on-premise should be based on a thorough analysis of the company's specific needs, resources, and strategic goals. Many organizations are taking a hybrid approach that combines the best of both worlds, using the cloud for certain applications and maintaining other critical AI systems on on-premises servers. This flexible approach allows businesses to benefit from the benefits of the cloud, while ensuring security and control over sensitive data.

Chapter 7: Planning and Execution of AI Projects

Planning and executing AI projects is a process that requires a strategic and methodical approach. As companies begin to integrate AI solutions into their operations, it is essential to establish a robust framework that ensures the success of the project. This chapter addresses the definition of objectives and scopes of an AI project, the calculation of return on investment (ROI), AI-specific project management strategies, and the success and monitoring metrics that help evaluate the performance of these projects.

Defining the objectives and scope of an AI project

Defining **goals and scopes** is the crucial first step in planning an AI project. Without a clear understanding of what is to be achieved, efforts can be dispersed and result in ineffective implementation. Goals should be specific, measurable, achievable, relevant, and time-bound (SMART). For example, a company could set a goal of improving operational efficiency by 20% by automating customer service processes through an AI chatbot within six months.

The scope of the project, on the other hand, defines the boundaries and expectations of the work. This includes identifying which specific processes will be affected, what resources will be needed, and what the duration of the project will be. A well-defined scope helps avoid **"scope leakage,"** where new requirements or changes are continually added that can divert the project from its initial goals. To do this, it is advisable to involve all stakeholders from the beginning, making sure that their needs are understood and aligned with the project's objectives.

Additionally, it is critical to conduct a feasibility analysis to assess the project's alignment with the company's overall strategy. This involves examining whether the technology and resources available are suitable for the type of implementation being sought, as well as identifying any potential obstacles that may arise. Once the goals and scope have been established, you can begin to develop a detailed plan that guides the execution of the AI project.

Return on Investment (ROI) Calculation in AI

Calculating **return on investment (ROI)** is an essential component of any AI project, as it allows companies to assess the financial viability of deploying smart technologies. Not only does this analysis help justify the initial investment, but it also provides a framework for measuring the impact of AI on the organization over time.

To calculate ROI, companies should start by **defining the costs associated with the project**, which can include investment in technology, staff training, consulting, and maintenance. To these costs must be added the time that the team will spend on the development and implementation of the solution. Once you have a clear view of the costs, it is essential to project the **benefits that are expected to be obtained**. These benefits can be tangible, such as increased revenue through improved sales thanks to an optimized recommendation system, or intangible, such as improved customer satisfaction or reduced wait times.

The ROI calculation can be expressed as follows:

$$ROI = \frac{(Benefits - Costs)}{Costs} \times 100$$

This percentage provides a clear view of the effectiveness of the investment. A positive ROI indicates that the benefits outweigh the costs, while a negative ROI indicates that the investment has not been profitable. However, it is important to note that the benefits of AI may not be immediate, and many times manifest themselves in the long term. As such, companies should establish a time horizon for evaluating ROI that considers both immediate benefits and long-term benefits.

AI Project Management Strategies

Project **management in AI** requires a specialized approach, given the complexity and technical nature of these projects. Unlike traditional projects, which may follow a more linear approach, AI projects often require an agile approach that allows them to adapt to changes in data, technology, or business requirements.

An effective strategy for AI project management is to implement agile methodologies, such as **Scrum or Kanban**, that encourage continuous collaboration and iterative improvement. These methodologies allow teams to work in short cycles, known as sprints, where they can develop prototypes and receive constant feedback from stakeholders. Not only does this approach improve the quality of the final product, but it also increases customer and team satisfaction by involving everyone in the decision-making process.

In addition, it is vital to have a **multidisciplinary team** that combines technical and business skills. This includes data scientists, software engineers, business analysts, and industry experts, who can bring different perspectives and make sure the project is aligned with the organization's strategic goals. Collaboration and constant communication between team members are essential to the success of the project.

Risk **management** also plays a crucial role in the execution of AI projects. Identifying potential risks early on and establishing mitigation plans allows companies to anticipate issues and respond proactively. This is especially relevant in the field of AI, where data quality and ethics in the use of technology are factors that can significantly affect the outcome of the project.

Monitoring and success metrics for AI projects

Monitoring **and success metrics** are critical to evaluating the performance of AI projects and ensuring that set goals are met. Establishing key performance indicators (KPIs) allows organizations to measure the impact of AI on their operations and adjust strategies as needed.

KPIs should be aligned with the objectives of the project and can vary depending on the nature of the project. For example, if the goal is to improve operational efficiency, KPIs could include metrics such as reduced response time, increased productivity, or decreased costs. For projects focused on improving the customer experience, metrics could include customer satisfaction, retention rate, or Net Promoter Score (NPS).

It is important not only to measure performance in terms of results, but also to assess the quality of the AI model. This involves monitoring the model's accuracy, error rate, and generalizability, ensuring that the model works effectively in different scenarios and with unseen data.

The **analysis of the results obtained** allows companies to make adjustments and improvements in real time. Not only does this help optimize the performance of the AI model, but it also provides valuable insights that can influence future strategic decisions. Finally, it is essential to foster a culture of continuous learning within the organization, where failures and successes are analyzed to draw lessons and constantly improve AI initiatives.

In short, AI project planning and execution is a complex process that requires meticulous attention to goals, costs, management strategies, and success metrics. By addressing each of these elements holistically, companies can maximize the impact of their AI investments and ensure they align with their long-term strategic goals.

Chapter 8: AI in Marketing and Customer Experience

In today's business environment, where competition is fierce and consumer expectations are higher than ever, artificial intelligence (AI) has become a critical ally in optimizing marketing strategies and improving the customer experience. This chapter explores how AI transforms marketing and customer service through personalization, predictive analytics, campaign automation, and the use of chatbots and virtual assistants. As companies adopt these technologies, they are discovering new ways to connect with their customers and offer them more satisfying and relevant experiences.

Personalizing the customer experience with AI

Personalization is one of the most exciting promises that AI brings to marketing and customer experience. Instead of applying a "one-size-fits-all" approach, companies can use AI to tailor their communication and offerings to each customer's individual needs. This is achieved by analyzing large volumes of data that capture consumer behaviors, preferences, and buying patterns.

AI algorithms allow businesses to segment their audience in much more granular ways, identifying specific groups within their customer base and offering content, products, and services that resonate with their particular interests. For example, platforms such as **Netflix** and **Spotify** use AI to recommend movies, series or music based on users' consumption history. This personalization not only improves the customer experience, but also increases loyalty and engagement, as consumers feel that brands understand and respond to their preferences.

In addition, personalization also extends to communication. Through AI, businesses can send more relevant marketing messages at the right time, thereby increasing conversion rates. For example, using machine learning techniques, systems can predict when a customer is most likely to open an email or interact with an offer, maximizing the effectiveness of campaigns.

Using AI in personalization also allows businesses to go beyond recommendations. Sentiment analysis tools can analyze social media comments and reviews to understand how customers feel about the brand and tailor communication accordingly. In this sense, AI not only helps to better understand customers, but also allows us to build more meaningful and lasting relationships.

Predictive Analytics for Marketing

Predictive analytics is another area where AI is revolutionizing marketing. This technique uses statistical models and machine learning algorithms to analyze historical data and predict future consumer behaviors and trends. By anticipating what customers are likely to do next, businesses can make more informed and strategic decisions.

For example, through predictive analytics, a company can identify which customers are most likely to make a purchase, thus allowing targeted marketing efforts to be directed towards these individuals. It can also help identify products that a customer might be interested in buying based on their past behaviors, increasing the likelihood that they will make a purchase.

In addition, predictive analytics is used to **optimize ad spend**. AI advertising platforms can analyze the performance of different campaigns and automatically adjust strategies in real-time, redirecting the budget towards the ads that are driving the most conversions. This allows businesses to maximize their return on investment (ROI) by ensuring that every dollar spent on marketing is being used as effectively as possible.

Predictive analytics can also help businesses manage the **customer lifecycle**. By predicting when a customer may lose interest or stop buying, businesses can implement retention strategies, such as personalized promotions or loyalty programs, before the customer leaves the brand. Not only does this improve retention, but it also optimizes customer lifetime value (CLV), a crucial indicator for the financial health of any business.

Ad campaign automation and targeting

Ad campaign automation is a growing trend driven by AI, which allows businesses to execute and optimize campaigns more efficiently. AI-based automation tools can manage ad buying and placement in real-time, adjusting strategies based on performance and target audience segmentation.

One of the most effective applications of automation is the use of **bidding systems** that allow advertisers to bid on ad space based on customer data. These tools analyze factors such as user behavior, time of day, and location in real-time to determine the best bid strategy and maximize ad exposure to the right people at the right time. This reduces wasted resources and ensures that ads are shown to the most relevant segments.

Additionally, automation allows businesses to **personalize advertising experiences** across multiple channels, from emails to social media. For example, systems can automatically send personalized emails to customers based on their previous interactions with the brand, improving the open and conversion rate.

Segmentation, facilitated by AI, has also evolved significantly. Instead of relying on basic demographic criteria, businesses can use data analytics to segment their customers based on more complex behaviors and preferences. This allows them to create more effective campaigns that resonate with different groups, increasing marketing effectiveness and customer satisfaction.

Examples of chatbots and virtual assistants in customer service

Chatbots and virtual assistants have emerged as fundamental tools in customer service, offering instant answers and improving the customer experience. Equipped with AI and natural language processing (NLP), these systems can understand and respond to queries in a human-like manner, allowing businesses to provide 24/7 customer service.

A notable example is **Zendesk**, which offers chatbot solutions that can be integrated into websites and apps. These chatbots are capable of answering frequently asked questions, managing service requests, and guiding customers through purchasing processes, all without human intervention. Not only does this improve operational efficiency by freeing up human agents to focus on more complex queries, but it also provides a seamless experience for customers, who can get instant answers at any time of the day.

Another success story is **Sephora**, which has implemented a virtual assistant called Sephora Virtual Artist. This assistant allows customers to try on different makeup products through augmented reality, providing a personalized experience that connects AI with online shopping. By interacting with the assistant, customers can receive product recommendations based on their skin tone and preferences, improving the shopping experience and increasing conversions.

These examples illustrate how chatbots and virtual assistants not only help businesses streamline their customer service processes, but also enrich the customer experience by offering more personalized and efficient interactions. With the continued evolution of AI, the use of these technologies in customer service is likely to continue to grow, allowing businesses to stay competitive in an ever-changing market.

In conclusion, artificial intelligence is redefining marketing and customer experience, allowing businesses to personalize interactions, predict behaviors, automate campaigns, and improve customer service. By adopting these technologies, organizations not only position themselves to compete in a saturated market, but they also create more meaningful relationships with their customers, resulting in greater long-term satisfaction and loyalty. Implementing AI in these key areas isn't just a competitive advantage; it is a strategic imperative for success in the twenty-first century.

Chapter 9: AI in Finance and Risk Analysis

Artificial intelligence is transforming the financial industry, providing powerful tools for risk prediction, assessment, and management. As financial institutions face an ever-changing environment, the ability to use AI to streamline processes and improve decision-making becomes crucial. This chapter explores AI models for financial prediction, risk assessment and mitigation, fraud detection, and investment optimization.

AI models for financial forecasting

AI models for financial forecasting are essential tools that allow organizations to analyze historical data and extract meaningful patterns to foresee future trends. These models use machine learning and deep learning techniques to process huge volumes of data from various sources, such as financial statements, economic news, and social media. In doing so, they provide more accurate forecasts on asset performance, market trends, and consumer behaviors.

One of the most prominent applications of these models is in **the prediction of stock prices**. Using regression algorithms and recurrent neural networks (RNNs), analysts can identify past trends in prices and predict future market movements. Not only are these predictions valuable for traders and investment analysts, but they also allow companies to plan long-term business strategies based on realistic projections.

In addition, AI models can be used for **bankruptcy prediction**. Through the creation of credit scoring models, financial institutions can assess the likelihood that a company will not be able to meet its financial obligations. This is achieved by analyzing key indicators, such as debt-to-equity ratios and cash flows, and comparing them with historical data from companies that have filed for bankruptcy. By identifying at-risk companies, institutions can make more informed decisions about lending and portfolio management.

AI's ability to adapt and learn from new data is also a critical factor. As more data is generated and market conditions change, AI models can be adjusted and recalibrated to remain accurate. This ensures that predictions are not only relevant in the present, but also remain useful in an ever-evolving future.

Risk assessment and mitigation using AI

Risk **assessment and mitigation** is a critical function in finance, where wrong decisions can result in significant losses. AI offers advanced tools to analyze risks more effectively and proactively. Using machine learning algorithms, financial institutions can identify patterns in data that could signal the emergence of risks before they materialize.

A key application of AI in this context is **credit risk management**. AI models can analyze information from potential customers, including their banking transactions, payment history, and financial behavior, to assess the likelihood of default. Not only does this improve the accuracy of credit decisions, but it also allows institutions to set tighter credit limits, which in turn reduces the risk of losses due to defaults.

AI is also being used to manage **market risk**, where unexpected changes in market conditions can cause significant volatility. Through predictive models and time series analysis, institutions can simulate different market scenarios and their potential impacts on their portfolios. This allows them to develop more effective hedging strategies and respond more nimbly to sudden changes in the financial environment.

Operational **risk assessment** is another area where AI has shown a positive impact. By analyzing behavior patterns and processes within the organization, AI can identify vulnerabilities that could result in financial loss or reputational damage. Institutions can then implement controls and mitigation measures before incidents occur, creating a safer and more efficient work environment.

Fraud detection and transaction monitoring

Fraud **detection** is one of the fields where artificial intelligence has made a noticeable difference. As online and mobile transactions have increased, so has the sophistication of fraud methods. Traditional systems often can't keep up with the speed and complexity of new tactics used by fraudsters. However, AI systems, trained on large datasets of historical transactions, can identify suspicious patterns and anomalous behavior in real time.

For example, machine learning algorithms can analyze transactions in real-time and assess their risk based on various factors, such as the user's geographic location, transaction amount, and customer history. If a transaction seems out of the ordinary, the system can flagify the activity for further review or even stop the transaction automatically, thus protecting the institution and its customers from potential fraud.

In addition, AI is not only used to detect fraud once it occurs, but it can also help **prevent** future fraud. Through continuous data analysis, these systems can learn and adapt to new tactics used by criminals. This means that, over time, they become more effective at identifying emerging threats, significantly reducing the risk of fraud.

Transaction monitoring is equally crucial, especially in highly regulated environments such as the banking sector. Institutions must adhere to strict **know-your-customer** (KYC) and **anti-money**

laundering (AML) standards. AI facilitates this process by automating the collection and analysis of customer data, allowing institutions to identify and report suspicious transactions more efficiently.

Investment optimization with AI

Investment **optimization** is another area where artificial intelligence is changing the rules of the game. Fund managers and investors use AI models to identify investment opportunities that may not be apparent through traditional methods. These models can process a staggering amount of data, from financial reports and market trends to real-time news and social media, to generate more informed investment recommendations.

A prominent use of AI in this area is **algorithmic trading**, where algorithms can make trades in milliseconds, making decisions based on data patterns that are imperceptible to humans. This allows traders to take advantage of market opportunities before they are recognized by other investors, thus maximizing the potential return. The speed and accuracy of these automated transactions are vital in an environment where every second counts.

In addition, AI can be used to **optimize the allocation of assets** in a portfolio. By analyzing historical data and simulating different market scenarios, models can recommend how to allocate capital across different asset classes to minimize risk and maximize return. This is especially valuable in a volatile financial environment, where market conditions can change rapidly.

AI's ability to perform sentiment analysis also plays an important role in optimizing investments. By assessing market sentiment through social media data and news, investors can gain valuable insights into how public perceptions can influence asset prices. This information can be crucial for making informed decisions about when to buy or sell.

In conclusion, artificial intelligence is revolutionizing finance and risk analysis by providing advanced tools for prediction, evaluation, and management. From financial prediction models to fraud detection and investment optimization, AI enables financial institutions to be more efficient, accurate, and proactive in their decision-making. By adopting these technologies, organizations can not only improve their profitability and sustainability, but also strengthen their competitive position in an ever-changing financial world.

Chapter 10: AI in Human Resources and Talent Management

Artificial intelligence (AI) is radically transforming the way companies manage their human resources and talent. From recruitment automation to workplace climate analysis and employee retention, AI offers tools that not only streamline processes, but also enable organizations to create a more equitable and productive work environment. This chapter examines the applications of AI in human resources, addressing key topics such as recruitment and selection, performance evaluation, analysis of the work environment, and the use of chatbots for staff support.

Recruitment and selection with AI: Automation and ethical bias

Recruiting and recruiting are critical processes for the success of any organization, and AI has begun to play a vital role in optimizing these functions. AI tools can automate many administrative tasks, from reviewing resumes to scheduling interviews, allowing recruiters to focus on more strategic aspects of the selection process.

One of the main advantages of automation in recruitment is efficiency. AI systems can analyze hundreds of resumes in a matter of minutes, quickly identifying candidates who meet the set requirements. This speed not only speeds up the hiring process, but also allows companies to access a greater diversity of talent. By eliminating human bias in the first phase of screening, organizations can ensure that they are considering all potential candidates, regardless of their background.

However, implementing AI in recruitment is not without its challenges, especially when it comes to **ethical bias**. AI algorithms can learn and perpetuate existing biases if they are trained on data that contains bias. For example, if an AI model is primarily fed resumes of candidates from a specific demographic, it might favor candidates from that same group in future selections, excluding others equally qualified. This phenomenon, known as "algorithmic bias," has led organizations to question the fairness of their hiring processes and implement strategies to mitigate these risks.

To address these issues, companies need to take a proactive approach when developing their AI-based recruiting tools. This includes using diverse and representative data during model training, as well as implementing regular audits to evaluate and tune algorithms. Additionally, it's critical to maintain a balance between automation and human assessment, ensuring that recruiters continue to play an active role in final decision-making.

Performance Evaluation and Talent Development

Performance **appraisal** is one of the areas where AI can make a significant impact by providing more objective and accurate analytics. Traditionally, performance reviews have been subject to subjective biases, which can lead to unfair results and staff demotivation. AI, by integrating quantitative and qualitative metrics, allows for a more balanced and data-driven assessment.

AI systems can analyze employee performance through various metrics, including productivity indicators, goal fulfillment, and team contributions. These evaluations can be fed by real-time data from projects, communications, and sales results, providing a holistic view of an employee's performance. This approach not only improves the objectivity of assessments, but also makes it easier to identify areas for improvement and opportunities for professional development.

In addition, AI can play a crucial role in the **development of talent** within the organization. By analyzing performance data, companies can identify high-potential employees and create customized development programs that address their specific needs. This can include training, mentoring, and job rotation opportunities that help employees reach their full potential.

The implementation of **continuous feedback systems** is also facilitated by AI. Through platforms that allow for regular feedback collection, employees can receive constant feedback on their performance, fostering a culture of continuous improvement and professional development. Not only does this help employees grow, but it also improves job satisfaction and talent retention.

Analysis of work environment and employee retention

The **work environment** is a determining factor in employee satisfaction and retention, and AI is revolutionizing the way organizations can measure and improve this aspect. AI-powered workplace analytics tools allow companies to collect and analyze employee experience data more effectively.

By using surveys and analysis of online interaction data, companies can gain valuable insights into employees' perception of their work environment. These analyses may include identifying factors that contribute to dissatisfaction, such as lack of recognition, development opportunities, or communication problems. Through this data, organizations can implement strategic changes to improve the work environment, thus increasing employee satisfaction and engagement.

In addition, AI also helps companies predict **employee retention**. Predictive models can analyze patterns in staff turnover and pinpoint employees who are at risk of leaving the organization. By identifying these employees early, companies can take proactive steps to address their concerns, offer incentives, and create a work environment that encourages their retention. Not only does this save costs associated with hiring and training new employees, but it also contributes to the creation of a strong and cohesive work culture.

Chatbots and assistants for staff support

Chatbots and virtual assistants are emerging as effective tools in human resource management, providing instant support to employees and facilitating communication within the organization. These AI systems can handle a variety of tasks, from answering frequently asked questions about company policies to helping employees access resources and benefits.

The implementation of chatbots in the area of human resources allows companies to offer a more agile and accessible employee service. For example, a chatbot can help an employee navigate the process of requesting days off, providing information about the vacation policy and making it easier to submit requests without the need to wait for a human to become available. Not only does this improve the employee experience, but it also reduces the workload for the HR team.

Additionally, chatbots can serve as a **data collection** tool, allowing businesses to gain valuable insights into their employees' concerns and needs. Through regular interactions, chatbots can identify trends in questions or issues raised by employees, allowing organizations to proactively address these topics.

Virtual assistants can also help foster a culture of continuous feedback, allowing employees to make inquiries about their performance and receive instant guidance on their professional development. This can be particularly useful in large organizations where the personal connection with the HR department may be limited.

In conclusion, artificial intelligence is reshaping the human resources and talent management landscape by offering tools that optimize recruitment processes, performance evaluation, work environment analysis, and staff support. By adopting these technologies, organizations can not only improve the efficiency of their operations, but also create a more inclusive, equitable, and talent-development-focused work environment. The successful implementation of AI in human resources is therefore an investment not only in technology, but also in human capital, which is the true engine of any organization.

Chapter 11: AI in Operations and Logistics

Artificial intelligence (AI) is revolutionizing the field of operations and logistics, allowing companies to be more efficient, reduce costs, and improve service quality. From supply chain optimization to inventory management and transportation, AI offers solutions that transform the way organizations manage their operations. This chapter delves into the applications of AI in supply chain, inventory management, route optimization, and the use of robotics in manufacturing.

Supply chain optimization with AI

The **supply chain** is a complex system that involves the coordination of multiple actors, from suppliers to end consumers. AI plays a crucial role in streamlining this process, improving visibility and agility at every stage. AI-powered systems can analyze large volumes of data in real-time, allowing businesses to make informed and quick decisions, adapting to market fluctuations and customer demands.

One of the most important aspects of supply chain optimization is **demand forecasting**. Using machine learning models, companies can analyze historical sales patterns and combine this information with external data, such as market trends, seasonal events, and economic conditions. This predictive analytics allows companies to anticipate product demand more accurately, minimizing the risk of overstock or stockouts.

AI also makes **supplier management** easier. Through algorithms that evaluate supplier performance based on key metrics such as lead time, product quality, and consistency, companies can select the best trading partners. In addition, AI systems can alert managers to potential supply chain disruptions, such as delivery delays or quality issues, allowing preventative measures to be taken before they become serious problems.

Another significant benefit is the improvement in **distribution logistics**. AI makes it possible to optimize resource allocation and production planning, helping to reduce costs and improve efficiency. By integrating real-time data from different sources, companies can improve their responsiveness to unforeseen situations, such as changes in demand or disruptions in transportation, resulting in a more resilient and efficient supply chain.

Application of AI in inventory management

Inventory **management** is one of the areas where AI can make a significant difference. Inefficient inventory management can lead to costly product surpluses or shortages, affecting profitability and customer satisfaction. AI provides advanced tools to optimize this process, allowing businesses to have a clearer and more accurate view of their inventory levels.

AI systems can analyze past sales data, buying patterns, and market trends to predict optimal inventory levels. This translates into **demand-driven inventory management**, where companies can adjust their stock levels according to the most accurate forecasts. For example, if an AI model indicates that a specific product will experience an increase in demand due to a market trend, the company can increase its stock accordingly, avoiding lost sales.

In addition, AI can help **optimize inventory replenishment**. Using algorithms that analyze lead time, storage costs, and turnover rates, companies can set automatic and strategic reorder levels that minimize the risk of overstock and associated costs. This not only improves operational efficiency, but also frees up capital that can be reinvested in other areas of the business.

Storage **automation** is another valuable application of AI in inventory management. Automated systems can monitor and manage inventory in real-time, allowing businesses to accurately track products in stock. This translates into a significant reduction in human error and more efficient management of storage spaces, which in turn contributes to improved productivity and reduced operating costs.

Route optimization and transportation management

Route **optimization** is a critical component of logistics and transportation, where fuel costs and delivery time are essential factors for profitability. AI offers advanced tools for route planning, using optimization algorithms that consider multiple variables, such as real-time traffic, weather conditions, and time constraints.

AI systems can analyze data in real-time to determine the most efficient route for each delivery. Not only does this reduce operating costs by minimizing fuel consumption and driving time, but it also improves customer satisfaction by ensuring faster and more predictable deliveries. For example, by using an AI-powered navigation system, a transportation company can dynamically adjust its routes based on traffic and other factors, avoiding unnecessary delays.

In addition, AI can help in **fleet management**, optimizing the allocation of vehicles and resources based on demand. Algorithms can analyze historical transportation data to predict fleet needs at different times of the day or week, allowing companies to plan more efficiently and reduce downtime costs.

The integration of AI with technologies such as the **Internet of Things** (IoT) is also revolutionizing transportation management. With sensors installed in vehicles, companies can collect real-time data on vehicle performance, charging status, and traffic conditions. This information can be analyzed by AI algorithms to improve logistics and route planning, further increasing operational efficiency.

Examples of robotics and AI in manufacturing

Robotics and artificial intelligence are interconnected in modern manufacturing, where together they are transforming production processes and improving operational efficiency. Smart factories, which use autonomous AI-powered robots, are proving to be more flexible and productive than ever before.

One of the most prominent applications of robotics in manufacturing is the use of **collaborative robots**, or cobots, that work alongside human employees. These robots can perform repetitive and physically demanding tasks, allowing workers to focus on more complex and creative activities. For example, on a production line, a robot may be responsible for assembling components while a worker takes care of quality monitoring and fine-tuning, improving overall productivity.

In addition, AI is enabling the **automation of quality control** in manufacturing. By using computer vision systems and machine learning algorithms, factories can inspect products in real-time to detect defects. Not only does this increase the accuracy of quality control, but it also reduces the time needed for inspection, resulting in more efficient production.

AI systems are also revolutionizing **production planning and scheduling**. Using predictive models, companies can anticipate problems on the production line, such as interruptions or delays in the supply of materials. This allows for more dynamic and adaptable scheduling, where production can be adjusted in real-time to optimize performance and minimize costs.

Finally, robotics and AI are driving the development of **autonomous factories**, where production processes are managed almost entirely automatically. These facilities use advanced algorithms to manage internal logistics, predictive maintenance of machinery and task scheduling, creating a highly efficient and adaptive production environment.

In conclusion, artificial intelligence is redefining operations and logistics by offering innovative solutions that optimize supply chain, inventory management, route planning, and manufacturing. By adopting these technologies, businesses can improve their operational efficiency, reduce costs, and increase customer satisfaction. Successfully implementing AI in these fields not only provides a competitive advantage, but also prepares organizations for a future where adaptability and innovation are essential for success.

Chapter 12: AI in Innovation and Product Development

Artificial intelligence (AI) is revolutionizing the way companies approach **innovation and product development**, offering tools and approaches that accelerate product creation and improve responsiveness to market demands. From rapid prototyping to demand forecasting to assisted design, AI enables companies to not only develop products more efficiently, but also innovate in ways that were previously unimaginable. This chapter explores how AI is transforming the product development lifecycle, facilitating disruptive innovation and adaptation to an ever-changing market environment.

Rapid prototyping and simulation using AI

Rapid **prototyping** has been a crucial component in product development, allowing companies to create initial versions of their products quickly and efficiently. With the addition of artificial intelligence, this process has reached new heights, making it easier to simulate and optimize prototypes before they are physically produced.

AI systems can analyze a vast amount of data and simulate different performance scenarios for a new product. For example, by using **generative design** simulations, companies can evaluate multiple configurations and materials in a virtual environment. Not only does this speed up the design process, but it also reduces the costs associated with producing physical prototypes. By conducting virtual testing, organizations can identify potential problems and make adjustments before time and resources are invested in manufacturing a final product.

In addition, AI enables the integration of **predictive models** into the prototyping process. By using data from past markets and consumer trends, developers can predict how consumers will react to different features of a product. This means that businesses can focus on features that will truly resonate with their audience, thus eliminating uncertainty in the development process. This methodology not only shortens the time to market, but also increases the chances of product success.

AI's simulation capabilities extend to **product lifecycle assessment** as well. Developers can simulate the use of the product in real-world conditions, allowing for a better understanding of its durability and functionality. This is especially valuable in industries such as automotive, electronics, and consumer goods, where customer expectations for quality and reliability are extremely high.

AI for demand forecasting and product planning

Demand **forecasting** is one of the most complex challenges companies face in product development. A mistake at this stage can result in overproduction of a product that will not sell, or an inability to meet market demand, which can lead to customer dissatisfaction. AI offers powerful tools to address this challenge, improving the accuracy of predictions and enabling more effective product planning.

Machine learning **models** can analyze historical sales data, market trends, and consumer behaviors to identify patterns that might go unnoticed by human analysts. By integrating variables such as seasonality, past promotions, and competitor analysis, businesses can get much more accurate demand forecasts. This approach not only improves responsiveness to changes in demand, but also optimizes resource allocation and inventory management.

AI can also help in **product lifecycle planning**. By analyzing real-time data and emerging trends, companies can make informed decisions about when to launch a new product, when to make upgrades, and when to discontinue products that are no longer profitable. This ability to adapt is critical in a rapidly evolving market, where speed and agility are crucial to success.

In addition, **artificial intelligence** can assist in market segmentation and the identification of product niches. By analyzing demographic and behavioral data, companies can uncover untapped market opportunities, allowing them to develop products that meet specific consumer needs. This not only creates more relevant and personalized products, but also contributes to a sustainable competitive advantage.

AI-Aided Design Applications

AI-assisted design is emerging as a game-changer in the product development process. AI-powered design tools enable designers to create, evaluate, and modify products with unprecedented speed and accuracy. Not only do these applications improve design quality, but they also encourage innovation by facilitating experimentation and iteration.

One of the most fascinating applications of AI-aided design is the use of **generative design algorithms**. These tools allow designers to enter parameters such as materials, costs, and manufacturing constraints, and then the AI automatically generates multiple design options that meet these requirements. Not only does this approach expand creative possibilities, but it also helps designers find solutions they might not have considered, thus driving innovation.

AI-assisted design can also optimize product **ergonomics** and functionality. By analyzing how users interact with products under various conditions, AI tools can provide recommendations to improve usability and customer experience. For example, in the automotive industry, AI can simulate the behavior of users in a vehicle and suggest adjustments to the interior design to improve comfort and accessibility.

In addition, AI can be integrated into the **design validation** process. By using data from previous prototypes and performance analysis, AI systems can predict how a new design will perform in the market, allowing companies to make informed decisions about adjustments before launch. This ability to anticipate potential problems and opportunities not only saves time and resources, but also increases the likelihood of success of the final product.

Disruptive innovation with AI in new product development

Disruptive **innovation** is a phenomenon in which new technologies or approaches transform markets and create new opportunities. AI is at the heart of this transformation, enabling companies to not only develop innovative products, but also redefine how these products are created and delivered to the market.

Companies are using AI to **identify emerging trends** and innovation opportunities more effectively. By analyzing large data sets from social media, product reviews, and shopping behaviors, organizations can spot shifts in consumer preferences before they become mainstream trends. This allows companies to get ahead of the competition by developing products that meet emerging consumer needs.

AI also enables the creation of **intelligent products**, which not only fulfill a basic function, but also adapt and evolve based on user interaction. For example, smart appliances can learn from consumers' usage habits and adjust their operation to maximize energy efficiency. This approach not only improves the customer experience, but also opens up new opportunities for monetization through data-driven services.

The integration of AI into product development also fosters a **culture of continuous innovation** within organizations. As companies adopt AI technologies, they become more agile and responsive to market changes. This creates a cycle in which innovation becomes an integral part of the business strategy, driving not only the development of new products, but also the continuous improvement of existing ones.

In short, artificial intelligence is transforming the field of innovation and product development, allowing companies to accelerate their processes, anticipate market demands, and design products more effectively. From rapid prototyping to demand forecasting to assisted design, AI not only improves efficiency, but also drives disruptive innovation, enabling organizations to adapt and thrive in an ever-evolving competitive environment. The integration of AI into product development is therefore an essential component for any company looking to lead in its industry and meet the needs of its customers effectively.

Part IV: Challenges and Ethical Considerations in AI

Artificial intelligence (AI) has significantly transformed the way businesses operate, offering unprecedented opportunities for innovation, efficiency, and growth. However, with these advances come significant challenges and ethical considerations that cannot be overlooked. This fourth part of the book focuses on the critical aspects surrounding the implementation of AI in business, exploring the ethical concerns and challenges associated with the use of this technology.

The adoption of AI raises deep questions about **accountability** and **transparency** in automated decision-making. How data is collected, processed, and used is critical to ensuring that AI applications are fair, equitable, and accountable. The potential for bias in algorithms, as well as the potential for negative impacts on the privacy and rights of individuals, underscore the need to address ethical implications proactively. Organizations need to be aware that their AI-related decisions not only affect their internal operations, but also their customers, employees, and society as a whole.

Additionally, in a world where consumer expectations and government regulation are constantly evolving, businesses need to take a responsible and ethical approach to AI. This involves not only complying with existing laws and regulations, such as GDPR and CCPA, but also anticipating future expectations and emerging standards in the realm of AI ethics. A company's ability to navigate these challenges not only impacts its reputation, but it can also determine its long-term success.

Throughout this part, fundamental topics such as data management and privacy, accountability in automated decision-making, bias and fairness in algorithms, as well as the social implications of automation and job displacement will be addressed. By exploring these topics, readers are expected to develop a deeper understanding of the need to integrate ethics into the design and implementation of AI solutions. AI has the potential to be a positive force for innovation and progress, but only if it is handled with careful consideration of its ethical and societal implications.

Chapter 13: Data Management and Privacy in AI Projects

Artificial intelligence (AI) feeds on data. The quality and quantity of this data is critical to the success of any AI project, as it directly influences the accuracy and effectiveness of the models. However, with the exponential growth in data collection and use, comes a set of critical challenges related to **privacy and data management**. This chapter explores the importance of data quality and security in AI projects, as well as relevant regulations and best practices to ensure data privacy and protection.

The importance of data quality and security

Data quality is a key aspect in the field of artificial intelligence. Without high-quality data, even the most advanced and sophisticated algorithms can produce erroneous or biased results. Low-quality data can result in the wrong business decisions, which can have significant consequences for organizations and their customers. Therefore, ensuring data quality involves a number of practices ranging from collecting and storing to processing and using that data.

One of the essential aspects of data quality is its **accuracy**. The data must be correct and accurately reflect reality so that AI models can make valid inferences. In addition, **completeness** is crucial; datasets that are incomplete can lead to models that do not adequately capture the complexity of the problem they are trying to solve. Consistency is also important, as data must be consistent and compatible over time and between different sources.

On the other hand, **data security** is an equally crucial aspect, as the increasing reliance on data has led to an increase in the risks of cyberattacks and data breaches. Organizations must implement robust security measures to protect the integrity and confidentiality of the data they use for their AI projects. This includes implementing access controls, data encryption, and training employees in cybersecurity practices. The combination of quality and security in data management not only ensures the success of AI projects, but also builds consumer trust and business reputation.

Privacy and data protection laws (GDPR, CCPA)

The legal framework that regulates the collection and use of data is constantly evolving, driven by growing concerns about privacy and the protection of personal data. Two of the most influential pieces of legislation in this area are the European Union's **General Data Protection Regulation** (GDPR) and the **California Consumer Protection Act** (CCPA).

The **GDPR,** which came into force in May 2018, sets out rigorous guidelines on the collection and processing of personal data of EU citizens. This regulation gives individuals greater control over their data, including rights such as access, rectification and deletion of their personal data. For organizations that use AI, this means that they must ensure that any personal data used in their models is GDPR compliant. The consequences of failing to comply with these regulations can be severe, including significant fines and reputational damage.

The CCPA**, meanwhile,** focuses on protecting the privacy rights of consumers in California. This law gives consumers the right to know what personal data is being collected about them, as well as the right to opt out of the sale of their personal information. The CCPA represents an important step toward protecting consumer privacy and has influenced privacy legislation in other U.S. states. Companies developing AI projects in California must be particularly diligent in implementing data management practices that comply with this law.

Both regulations emphasize the importance of **transparency** and **accountability** in data management. Organizations must not only ensure that their data collection practices are legal, but they must also be transparent with users about how their data is being used. This is especially critical in the context of AI, where the use of data to train models may not always be apparent to end users.

Privacy Principles by Design

The concept of **privacy by design** has become a fundamental principle in data management, especially in the context of AI. This approach implies that privacy should be considered from the initial stages of AI project development, rather than being a mere aftermath. By integrating privacy into every phase of the project lifecycle, organizations can minimize risk and ensure they are complying with data protection regulations from the start.

The implementation of privacy by design principles includes the **privacy impact assessment** (PIA), which helps identify and mitigate potential risks in the collection and use of personal data. This assessment allows organizations to anticipate privacy issues before they occur and take proactive steps to address them. In addition, **clear protocols** for data management must be established that include security measures, access controls, and auditing processes.

Another key aspect is minimizing **data collection**. Instead of collecting large volumes of data indiscriminately, organizations should limit themselves to collecting only the information necessary for the specific purpose of their AI project. Not only does this help reduce the risks associated with managing personal data, but it also makes it easier to comply with privacy regulations.

In addition, the privacy-by-design approach encourages **staff training and awareness** of the importance of privacy and data protection. By educating employees on best practices and relevant regulations, organizations can cultivate a culture of accountability around data management, which in turn contributes to more effective implementation of AI projects.

Protocols for anonymization and management of sensitive data

Data **anonymization** is a key technique for ensuring data privacy and security in AI projects. By removing or modifying information that can identify specific individuals, organizations can use data for training and analysis without compromising individuals' privacy. This is especially relevant in the context of AI, where data is used to train models that can make inferences based on personal information.

There are several anonymization techniques, such as **pseudonymization**, where personal identifiers are replaced with a pseudonym, and **generalization**, which involves reducing the accuracy of data to protect the identity of individuals. However, it is critical for organizations to be aware that anonymization is not foolproof. With the advancement of data analysis techniques, there is a risk that seemingly anonymous data could be re-identified. Therefore, it is crucial to apply robust methods of anonymization and continuously evaluate the effectiveness of these methods.

Managing **sensitive data** is also a critical component in protecting privacy. Data such as medical information, religious beliefs, or sexual orientation are particularly sensitive and require careful handling. Organizations must implement strict policies for the collection, storage, and processing of this data, ensuring that all relevant regulations are complied with. This may include obtaining explicit consents from users before processing their sensitive data and implementing additional security controls.

Finally, creating an **incident response plan** is essential for any organization that handles personal data. This plan should detail how the company will respond to any data breach or security incident, including notifying the appropriate authorities and affected individuals. Proactive preparedness in this regard not only helps mitigate the impact of a potential incident, but also reinforces customer confidence that the organization is serious about data privacy and security.

In conclusion, data management and privacy are critical components in the implementation of artificial intelligence projects. As companies continue to adopt AI to improve their efficiency and competitiveness, it is critical that they also implement robust practices to ensure data quality, security, and privacy. Not only does this help to comply with regulations and avoid penalties, but it also strengthens consumer confidence and lays the foundation for responsible and ethical adoption of artificial intelligence in the future.

Chapter 14: Ethics and Responsibility in the Use of AI

Artificial intelligence has emerged as a transformative tool that, when used responsibly, can offer innovative solutions to complex problems in the business environment. However, the use of AI is not without ethical challenges that need to be addressed to ensure that its implementation benefits society as a whole. This chapter explores the intersection between ethics and responsibility in the use of AI, focusing on model biases, the need for transparency, the effects of AI on employment, and the creation of a robust ethical framework for its implementation.

Biases in AI Models: Causes and Solutions

Biases in AI models are one of the most discussed and critical issues in the field of artificial intelligence. These biases can arise from a variety of sources, such as the data used to train the models, feature selection, and algorithm design decisions. If training data reflects historical bias or discrimination, AI models can perpetuate and amplify these injustices, resulting in biased decisions that negatively affect specific groups of people. For example, recruitment systems that use historical data may dismiss candidates from underrepresented groups if that data does not reflect equitable representation.

To mitigate these biases, organizations must take a proactive approach to **reviewing and cleaning data**. This includes conducting bias audits, where the data used is evaluated to identify potential imbalances and biases. It is also essential to diversify data sources and ensure that datasets are representative of the diversity of the target population. In addition, involving multidisciplinary teams in the development of AI models can provide different perspectives that help identify and address biases that might otherwise be overlooked.

Another key strategy to combat bias is the **implementation of bias-tuning techniques** in algorithms. These techniques seek to balance the impact of biases on automated decisions. However, the fight against bias in AI is not limited to the technical aspects; it also requires an ethical commitment from organizations to ensure that their AI applications do not perpetuate inequities or cause harm to vulnerable communities.

Transparency in algorithms and social responsibility

Transparency in the development and implementation of AI algorithms is critical to building trust in this technology. As automated decisions increasingly impact our lives, from credit allocation to recruitment, it's crucial for organizations to be clear about how their AI models work and how they make decisions. The **"black box"** of AI algorithms, which makes it difficult to understand how decisions are reached, can lead to mistrust and the perception of unfairness.

Promoting transparency involves clearly documenting and communicating the criteria used in the construction of the models, as well as the training data used. Additionally, organizations can adopt **external auditing** practices, where algorithms are reviewed by third parties to ensure they are operating fairly and responsibly. Not only does this transparency help mitigate mistrust, but it also fosters a culture of **social responsibility**, where companies feel compelled to act in the best interests of their users and society at large.

Social responsibility also extends to how organizations address the social impact of their technologies. By considering the implications of their decisions in the development of AI-based products and services, companies can position themselves as responsible leaders in technological innovation. This involves not only compliance with regulations, but also an active commitment to making positive contributions to the community and addressing the potential negative effects that AI may have on society.

AI and the Future of Work: Effects on Employment

The impact of AI on the labor market is a topic that generates great debate. As companies adopt AI to automate tasks and streamline processes, concerns arise that this could lead to job losses in certain industries. However, the scenario is more complex; while it's true that some jobs could disappear, AI also has the potential to create new opportunities and transform existing roles.

The key to meeting this challenge lies in **adaptation and training**. Organizations should invest in training their staff to equip them with the skills needed to work alongside AI. This includes not only AI-related technical skills, but also interpersonal and critical thinking skills that will be increasingly valued in an ever-changing work environment. Collaboration between humans and machines can result in a more efficient and nurturing work environment, where employees can focus on higher value-added tasks while AI handles repetitive and routine tasks.

In addition, it is critical that governments and educational institutions join this effort, providing training and reskilling programs that prepare the workforce for the future. This proactive approach can mitigate the negative impact of automation and contribute to a more equitable transition to a more technology-focused labor market.

Ethical Framework for the Implementation of AI in Business

To ensure that the implementation of AI in business is ethical and responsible, it is necessary to establish an **ethical framework** that guides the development and use of this technology. This framework must be based on principles of equity, responsibility, transparency and respect for human rights. Organizations must commit to developing clear policies that address ethical concerns related to AI, establishing standards and guidelines that promote the responsible use of technology.

A key component of this framework is the **creation of a code of conduct** for the use of AI, detailing the expectations and responsibilities of everyone involved in the development and implementation of AI solutions. This code must be accessible and understandable to all employees and stakeholders, fostering a culture of ethics and responsibility in the organization.

In addition, it is essential to establish **oversight mechanisms** that allow the impact of AI solutions on society and the work environment to be continuously assessed. This can include regular audits of AI models, as well as implementing feedback processes that allow employees and customers to voice their AI-related concerns and experiences.

Ultimately, an ethical and responsible approach to AI will not only benefit organizations and their customers, but will also contribute to building a more equitable and just society, where technology is used for the common good. By integrating ethics into AI implementation, companies can lead by example, demonstrating that it is possible to innovate responsibly and sustainably.

Part V: Practical Guide to Implementing AI Projects

Chapter 15: Step-by-Step Implementation Examples

Implementing artificial intelligence (AI) projects may seem like a monumental challenge, but breaking down the process into clear, structured steps can make it easier to transition from theory to practice. This chapter provides concrete examples of AI implementation in different business areas, illustrating how organizations can benefit from these technologies effectively and efficiently. We will explore the implementation of a customer service chatbot, a product recommendation model for e-commerce, the automation of human resources processes, and a sales prediction model.

Implementing a Customer Service Chatbot

Implementing a customer service chatbot is a practical example that can revolutionize the way businesses interact with their customers. The first step in this process is to define the purpose and functionalities of the chatbot. Should I be able to answer frequently asked questions, manage bookings, or help with troubleshooting? Once this is established, a dataset should be collected that includes common questions and answers, as well as examples of customer interactions.

Step 1: Selecting the Development Platform Choosing the right platform is crucial. There are various tools and platforms that allow the creation of chatbots without the need for extensive programming, such as Chatbot.com, Microsoft Bot Framework or Google Dialogflow. These tools offer intuitive interfaces and resources for training the model.

Step 2: Training the model Once the platform has been selected, the model must be trained. This involves uploading the collected data and using natural language processing (NLP) techniques to teach the chatbot to understand and respond appropriately to user questions. The quality of model formation will depend to a large extent on the diversity and quantity of the data provided.

Step 3: Testing and Adjustments After training the model, extensive testing should be done to ensure that the chatbot responds accurately and relevantly. This includes simulating conversations and evaluating the effectiveness of responses. It is essential to make adjustments based on the results of these tests, correcting inappropriate answers or improving language understanding.

Step 4: Implementation and Follow-up Once the chatbot has been trained and tested, it can be deployed on the company's website or app. However, implementation is not the end of the process; It is crucial to monitor the chatbot's performance and make regular updates. Collecting data on its use, as well as customer satisfaction, will allow continuous improvements to be made to the system.

Product recommendation model for e-commerce

Recommendation models are critical in the world of e-commerce, as they allow you to personalize the customer experience and increase sales. Implementing a recommendation model involves several steps, from data collection to model evaluation.

Step 1: Data collection and preparation The first step is to collect relevant data, such as purchase history, viewed products, and customer reviews. This data can be extracted from the e-commerce database. Next, the information should be cleaned and prepared, making sure that it is in a format suitable for analysis.

Step 2: Selecting the recommendation algorithm There are several types of recommendation algorithms, such as collaborative filtering and content-based filtering. Collaborative filtering uses data from similar users to offer recommendations, while content-based filtering analyzes product features to suggest similar items. The choice of algorithm will depend on the type of data available and the business objective.

Step 3: Training the model The next step is to train the model using the prepared data. This may require the use of machine learning tools such as TensorFlow or scikit-learn. During this phase, it is crucial to assess the accuracy of the model through cross-validation techniques.

Step 4: Integration into the e-commerce platform
Once the recommendation model has been trained and validated, it can be integrated into the e-commerce platform. It's important that recommendations are visible and accessible to users at the right time, such as on the homepage or during the checkout process.

Step 5: Monitoring and optimizationFinally, the performance of the recommendation model must be constantly monitored. Analyzing metrics such as click-through rate and conversion rate will help identify areas for improvement. Regularly updating the model with new data is crucial to maintaining the relevance of recommendations over time.

Automating HR processes with AI

Process automation in human resources (HR) is another powerful application of AI that can improve efficiency and effectiveness in talent management. This process starts with identifying tasks that can be automated, such as recruiting, performance management, and training.

Step 1: Identify processes to automate The first step is to carry out an analysis of current processes in HR to identify those areas that are repetitive and time-consuming. This can include resume collection, interview scheduling, and performance evaluation.

Step 2: Selecting Automation Tools There are a variety of automation tools and software that can be integrated with existing systems. Tools like **Workday** or **BambooHR** allow you to manage HR tasks more efficiently. Choosing the right tool will depend on the specific needs of the company and the compatibility with its technological infrastructure.

Step 3: Implementation and training Once the tools have been selected, the implementation must proceed. This includes software configuration and data migration from legacy systems. In addition, it is essential to train HR staff in the use of the new tools to ensure a smooth transition.

Step 4: Monitoring and Feedback Automation is not a one-time process. It is crucial to monitor the performance of automated processes and get feedback from staff on the effectiveness of new tools. This will allow for continuous adjustments and improvements.

Implementing a Sales Prediction Model

Sales prediction models are essential for businesses to anticipate market trends and make informed decisions. Implementing such a model involves several strategic steps.

Step 1: Collect Historical Data The first step in implementing a sales prediction model is to collect relevant historical data. This includes data on past sales, seasonality, promotions, and economic and market variables that may affect sales. The more information you have, the better the model will be.

Step 2: Exploratory Data Analysis Before building the model, it is important to perform an exploratory analysis of the data to identify patterns, correlations, and possible outliers. This will help to better understand the nature of the data and make informed decisions about how to proceed with modelling.

Step 3: Model selection and training There are several approaches to sales prediction, from classic statistical models such as linear regression to more advanced machine learning techniques. Selecting the right model will depend on the nature of the data and the company's goals. After selecting the model, it should be trained using historical data, adjusting the parameters to optimize its performance.

Step 4: Model Validation Once the model has been trained, it is crucial to validate it using a test dataset. This will help measure the accuracy of the predictions and make necessary adjustments before they are implemented in a real-world environment.

Step 5: Implementation and follow-up After validating the model, it can be implemented in the daily operation of the business. However, implementation should not be a static process; It is critical to monitor the model's performance over time and update it with new data to maintain its accuracy and relevance.

These examples illustrate how AI can be effectively implemented in various areas of business, from customer service to human resource management and sales prediction. Each implementation requires a structured and thoughtful approach, ensuring that AI solutions are not only effective, but also bring significant value to the organization and its customers. With a clear understanding of the steps to take, companies will be better prepared to embark on their journey to AI-powered digital transformation.

Chapter 16: Practical Tools and Resources

Implementing artificial intelligence in business not only requires a solid understanding of its concepts and techniques, but it is also essential to have the right tools and resources necessary to carry out successful projects. In this chapter, we will introduce a variety of tools, training platforms, and resources that will make it easier for companies to leverage AI. From software tools to learning communities, these resources are designed to equip organizations with what they need to start and scale their AI initiatives.

List of Free and Paid Tools for AI

The market offers a wide range of AI tools, both free and paid, that can be used for various applications, from data analysis to the development of machine learning models. Here are some of the most prominent tools in different categories:

1. **Data analysis and visualization tools**:
   - **Tableau**: A powerful data visualization tool that allows you to create interactive dashboards. It offers a limited free version and paid licenses.
   - **Power BI:** Developed by Microsoft, this tool allows companies to analyze data and share insights. It has a free version and paid options for advanced functionalities.

2. **Machine learning frameworks and libraries**:
   - **TensorFlow**: An open-source framework developed by Google that makes it easy to build and train deep learning models. It's free and very popular in the AI community.
   - **PyTorch**: Developed by Facebook, it is another deep learning library that stands out for its flexibility and ease of use, especially in research.

3. **Natural Language Processing (NLP) Tools**:
   - **SpaCy**: A natural language processing library in Python that is

fast and efficient, ideal for projects that require text analysis. It is open source and free.
- **Dialogflow**: A Google tool for building conversational interfaces, such as chatbots, that allows users to interact naturally. It has both free and paid options.

4. **Machine learning platforms**:
    - **H2O.ai**: It offers an open-source machine learning platform that allows users to develop AI models intuitively. H2O.ai provides both free and premium versions.
    - **DataRobot**: An automated machine learning platform that accelerates model development. It offers trial versions, but its full use is paid.

5. **Tools for deploying AI in the cloud**:
    - **Google Cloud AI:** Provides tools and APIs that allow businesses to integrate AI capabilities into their applications. It is based on a pay-as-you-go model.
    - **AWS AI Services**: Amazon Web Services offers a variety of AI

services, including speech recognition, translation, and image analytics, with a tiered pricing model.

Choosing the right tools will depend on the specific needs of each project, the budget available, and the skills of the team. Businesses should carefully evaluate each option and consider factors such as ease of use, support community, and scalability.

AI Training & Course Platforms for Enterprises

Training is an essential aspect for the successful implementation of AI projects. As the demand for AI skills grows, so do the opportunities to learn. Here are a few platforms that offer AI training courses and resources:

1. **Coursera**: Offers a wide variety of courses on AI and machine learning, taught by renowned universities and companies such as Stanford and Google. Courses typically include videos, readings, and hands-on assignments. They also offer specializations and certificate programs.
2. **edX**: Like Coursera, edX provides access to courses from prestigious institutions, with offerings ranging from introductions to AI to advanced programs in machine learning and data science. Most courses are free to access content, with a fee to earn certificates.
3. **Udacity**: Known for its **Nanodegrees**, Udacity offers intensive and specialized programs in AI, deep learning, and data analysis, designed in collaboration with leading companies. These programs are paid, but they provide in-depth, hands-on training.
4. **Kaggle**: More than a learning platform, Kaggle is a community where data scientists can participate in machine learning competitions. It offers tutorials and datasets to practice, and it's a great way to learn

through practice and collaboration with others.
5. **LinkedIn Learning**: Provides an extensive library of courses on AI, machine learning, and data analytics, with the advantage that users can learn at their own pace. It also offers a one-month free trial.
6. **Internal training platforms**: Some companies choose to develop internal training programs, where employees can learn about AI through workshops, seminars, and courses designed specifically for their needs. This fosters a culture of continuous learning and allows staff to align with the company's vision and goals.

Investing in staff training not only improves the technical competence of the team, but also creates an environment where innovation can thrive, maximizing the potential of AI in the organization.

Open resources and communities to learn and collaborate on AI

Collaboration and shared learning are fundamental in the field of artificial intelligence. There are numerous open resources and communities that foster cooperation and knowledge sharing:

1. **GitHub**: A platform that hosts open-source projects where developers can share and collaborate on AI tools and models. Many AI

libraries and tools are available here, making it easy to collaborate on projects.
2. **Kaggle**: In addition to being a space for competitions, Kaggle also has an active community where users can share kernels (code scripts) and learn from each other's approaches to data science and machine learning problems.
3. **Towards Data Science**: A Medium post where AI experts and enthusiasts share articles, tutorials, and case studies on various applications of AI and machine learning. It is an excellent resource for staying on top of the latest trends and discoveries in the field.
4. **AI Conferences and Meetups**: Attending AI conferences, webinars, and meetups provides valuable opportunities to learn from experts, network, and collaborate with other industry professionals. Events such as NeurIPS, ICML, and various local meetups are great for networking and knowledge acquisition.
5. **Online forums and communities**: Platforms like **Reddit, Stack Overflow,** and **AI Stack Exchange** are spaces where AI professionals can ask questions, share knowledge, and receive feedback. These forums are ideal for resolving doubts and learning from the experience of others.

Templates and guides for starting an AI project

To help companies take the first step in their AI initiatives, there are templates and how-to guides that can make project planning and execution easier. These tools are valuable for standardizing the process and ensuring that all critical aspects are addressed:

1. **AI Maturity Assessment Templates**: These templates allow businesses to assess their current level of AI adoption and identify areas for improvement. They include key questions and metrics that help establish a starting point.
2. **AI Project Planning Guides**: These guides cover all the steps required to implement an AI project, from defining goals to evaluating results. They include checklists and timelines that help keep the project on track.
3. **Templates for data management**: These tools help companies organize and document data collection, storage, and preparation, ensuring that the data used in AI models is of high quality and compliant with privacy regulations.
4. **Examples of AI use cases**: Providing examples of successful AI applications in different industries can inspire companies and offer them a reference on how to approach their own projects.

5. **Documentation of best practices**: Creating a repository of best practices and lessons learned from previous AI projects can be invaluable in guiding future efforts. This type of documentation can include technical aspects, ethical considerations, and tips on change management.

These templates and guides provide a structured framework that helps businesses navigate the complex process of implementing AI projects, maximizing their chances of success.

This chapter has provided a comprehensive overview of the practical tools and resources available for the implementation of AI projects in business. From specific tools and training platforms to learning communities and helpful templates, these resources are critical for organizations to confidently move forward on their AI journey. By leveraging these resources, companies can not only optimize their processes and improve their competitiveness, but also foster a culture of innovation and continuous learning that prepares them for the challenges of the future.

Conclusion

The implementation of artificial intelligence in business represents a monumental transformation that can redefine the way organizations operate and engage with their customers. Throughout this book, we have explored the significant benefits that AI can offer, as well as key strategies for its effective adoption and utilization. In this conclusion, it is critical to summarize these benefits, consider the future of AI in the business environment, and offer final tips to ensure a sustainable and successful adoption of this revolutionary technology.

Summary of Benefits and Key Strategies

AI has established itself as a fundamental tool to drive operational efficiency, improve decision-making and deliver personalized customer experiences. The benefits of AI are varied and span multiple areas, including process automation, advanced data analytics, and the ability to predict future trends. For example, companies that implement chatbots may see an increase in customer satisfaction and a reduction in operational costs, while freeing up human resources for more strategic tasks. In the realm of finance, AI enables organizations to perform more accurate risk analysis and detect fraud in real-time, resulting in safer and more efficient financial management.

However, to reap these benefits, it is crucial to adopt effective strategies. Organizations should start with a clear assessment of their AI maturity level, identify key areas where AI can have a significant impact, and set concrete, measurable goals. Creating an organizational culture that fosters innovation and continuous staff training is essential. By training employees in AI competencies, you not only increase their engagement, but you ensure that the technology is used effectively and ethically.

Collaboration between IT teams and business areas is also a key aspect. The synergy between these departments can facilitate the integration of AI solutions into existing processes, ensuring that the implementation is smooth and aligned with the company's strategic objectives. AI project management must be accompanied by constant monitoring, using appropriate metrics to evaluate success and make adjustments when necessary. In the end, the approach must be holistic, where AI is seen as an enabler of a broader transformation in the company's culture and operations.

Future of AI in Business and Next Steps

The future of AI in business is promising and full of opportunities. With continued advancements in machine learning, natural language processing, and computer vision, businesses can expect greater sophistication in AI applications. Personalization and automation will continue to evolve, allowing organizations to offer services and products that are further tailored to individual customer needs.

As AI becomes an integral part of business strategy, we are likely to see an increase in collaboration between humans and artificial intelligence. AI tools will not only be used to replace tasks, but also to enhance human capabilities, enhancing creativity and innovation. Companies that are able to integrate AI into their processes effectively will have a significant competitive advantage, as they will be able to adapt quickly to changes in the market and customer expectations.

However, this future also presents challenges. Organizations will need to navigate ethical issues related to the use of AI, including data privacy and fairness in algorithms. Corporate social responsibility will play an increasingly important role in how AI is implemented, and companies will need to be proactive in adopting practices that ensure ethical and responsible use of this technology. Next steps for organizations should include investing in research and development, as well as establishing governance frameworks that address these ethical challenges.

Final Tips for Sustainable AI Adoption

To ensure sustainable adoption of AI, it is essential that companies follow a few key recommendations:

1. **Continuing education and staff training**: Training is not a one-time event, but an ongoing process. Companies should establish training programs that keep employees up-to-date on the latest trends and technologies in AI, as well as best practices for their implementation.
2. **Develop a clear strategy**: Before jumping into AI implementation, it's vital to develop a strategy that clearly defines the goals, scope of the project, and the resources needed. This includes identifying specific use cases that align AI with the company's strategic goals.
3. **Foster a culture of innovation**: Innovation must be part of the organization's DNA. Companies should encourage their employees to experiment with and adopt new technologies, providing an environment where failure is seen as a learning opportunity.
4. **Commitment to ethics**: The adoption of AI must be accompanied by a serious commitment to ethical practices. Companies

must establish policies that ensure their algorithms are transparent and fair, and that customer data is handled responsibly.
5. **Monitoring and evaluation**: The implementation of AI does not end with its deployment. It is crucial to establish a monitoring system that allows the performance of AI solutions to be evaluated and adjustments to be made based on the results obtained. Success metrics should be clearly defined from the start.
6. **Collaboration with external experts**: Not all companies have the internal expertise needed to implement AI effectively. Collaborating with external consultants and experts can provide the expertise and perspective needed to overcome implementation challenges.

In summary, artificial intelligence offers transformative potential for business, but its successful adoption requires a strategic approach and a commitment to ethics and innovation. By following the recommendations and strategies presented in this book, companies will not only be well-equipped to implement AI, but they will also be able to take full advantage of the opportunities that this technology presents in an increasingly competitive business environment. With proper preparation and an open mindset towards change, the future of AI in business will not only be bright, but also sustainable.

Annexes

Glossary of technical terms

The field of artificial intelligence is full of technical terms and concepts that can be confusing for those who are new to this field. To facilitate the understanding and use of this book, a glossary of the most relevant terms is presented below:

- **Artificial Intelligence (AI):** A discipline of computer science that simulates human intelligence processes through algorithms and computational models, including learning, reasoning, and self-correction.
- **Machine Learning**: A subfield of AI that uses algorithms to allow machines to learn from data and improve their performance on specific tasks without being explicitly programmed.
- **Neural Networks**: Sets of algorithms inspired by the functioning of the human brain that are used to recognize patterns in data, crucial for classification and prediction tasks.
- **Natural Language Processing (NLP):** A branch of AI that enables computers to understand, interpret, and generate human language in meaningful ways.
- **Algorithm**: A set of defined rules or instructions that a machine follows to perform a specific task.

- **Data Mining**: The process of discovering patterns and relationships in large data sets using statistical and computational techniques.
- **Predictive Analytics**: Use of data, statistical algorithms, and machine learning to identify the likelihood of future outcomes based on historical data.
- **Algorithmic Bias**: A situation in which an algorithm produces results that are systematically unfair due to its design, the data used to train it, or the interpretation of its results.

Recommended bibliography

For those interested in delving into the study of artificial intelligence and its application in the business world, the following bibliography is recommended:

1. **"Artificial Intelligence: A Guide to Intelligent Systems"** by Michael Negnevitsky - A comprehensive text that provides an overview of the principles of AI and its applications.
2. **"Data Science for Business: What You Need to Know About Data Mining and Data-Analytic Thinking"** by Foster Provost and Tom Fawcett – This book explores how data science concepts apply to business and decision-making.
3. **"Superintelligence: Paths, Dangers, Strategies"** by Nick Bostrom - An in-depth exploration into the future implications of artificial intelligence on society and the economy.
4. **"Weapons of Math Destruction: How Big Data Increases Inequality and Threatens Democracy"** by Cathy O'Neil – A critical analysis of how algorithms can perpetuate bias and inequality in various areas.
5. **"The Fourth Industrial Revolution"** by Klaus Schwab – This book discusses how the convergence of technologies like AI is

transforming the business and social landscape.

Additional Case Studies

Case studies are a valuable tool for understanding how AI is implemented in the real world. Here are some additional examples illustrating successful applications of AI in various industries:

1. **Netflix**: The platform uses recommendation algorithms to personalize the viewing experience of its users, analyzing behavior patterns and preferences of viewers.
2. **Amazon**: With its product recommendation system, Amazon uses AI to analyze customers' purchase and browsing history, resulting in a more personalized shopping experience and often increased sales.
3. **IBM Watson**: This system has been used in the healthcare sector to aid in medical diagnoses, analyzing large volumes of clinical data and providing evidence-based recommendations.
4. **Zara**: The fashion chain has implemented AI systems to optimize its supply chain, allowing it to respond quickly to market trends and manage inventory more efficiently.
5. **Tesla**: The electric car company uses AI in its vehicles to improve autonomous driving functionality, collecting and analyzing data in real-time to adjust and improve their performance.

Self-assessment checklist for the implementation of AI in a company

To help organizations assess their readiness and advance the implementation of AI projects, the following checklist is presented:

1. **Maturity assessment**: What is the current level of AI adoption in the organization? Has a technology maturity assessment been conducted?
2. **Identification of application areas**: Have you identified the key areas where AI can be implemented to improve processes or generate value?
3. **Available resources**: Does the company have the talent to implement and maintain AI solutions? Is the right budget available?
4. **Organizational culture**: Are there cultural barriers that could hinder AI adoption? Is innovation and experimentation encouraged?
5. **Education and training**: Have training programs been established to train employees in the use and understanding of AI?
6. **Ethical assessment**: Have the ethical implications of AI implementation been considered? Have policies been put in place to address bias and ensure transparency?
7. **Monitoring and tuning**: Has a metrics system been defined to evaluate the

performance of AI solutions? Are regular reviews planned to make adjustments as needed?

Contact resources and AI communities

For those who wish to continue their education and connect with others interested in artificial intelligence, there are various online communities and resources. Here are some recommendations:

1. **AI Hub**: A platform that brings together AI professionals and resources to share knowledge and experiences.
2. **Kaggle**: An online community for data scientists where you can find competitions, datasets and discussion forums.
3. **Towards Data Science**: A Medium resource where AI and data analytics professionals share articles, tutorials, and guides.
4. **LinkedIn Groups**: There are multiple groups on LinkedIn dedicated to artificial intelligence and its application in business, where members share resources and discuss trends.
5. **Meetup**: A platform that allows AI professionals to organize and attend events and talks on artificial intelligence in various locations.
6. **Reddit**: Subreddits like r/MachineLearning and r/artificial can be great places to learn about and discuss the latest trends and technologies in AI.

With these appendices, a set of valuable resources is provided that not only complement the book's content, but also invite readers to further explore and learn in the fascinating world of artificial intelligence in business.

Here is an extensive list of artificial intelligence (AI) tools that can be implemented in various areas of business. Each tool includes a description, functions, utilities and the sectors in which it can be used.

1. IBM Watson

- **Description**: IBM's AI platform that enables companies to build artificial intelligence applications.
- **Functions**: Natural language processing, data analysis, machine learning, computer vision.
- **Utilities**: Implementation in areas such as customer service (chatbots), sentiment analysis, business process optimization.
- **Sectors**: Healthcare, finance, retail, telecommunications.

2. Google Cloud AI

- **Description**: A set of AI tools and services available through the Google cloud.
- **Features**: APIs for computer vision, natural language processing, machine translation, and speech recognition.
- **Utilities**: Improvement of user applications, data analysis, process automation.
- **Industries**: Marketing, customer service, data analysis.

3. Microsoft Azure AI

- **Description**: Microsoft's AI services platform that provides solutions for the development of intelligent applications.
- **Features**: Machine learning, computer vision, natural language processing, and bot services.
- **Utilities**: Creation of intelligent applications, data analysis, process automation.
- **Sectors**: Health, education, retail, manufacturing.

4. Salesforce Einstein

- **Description**: AI built into the Salesforce platform that improves customer relationship management (CRM).
- **Features**: Sales predictions, personalized recommendations, task automation.
- **Utilities**: Improved customer experience, optimization of sales processes.
- **Industries**: Sales, marketing, customer service.

5. Hootsuite Insights

- **Description**: Social media management tool that includes AI-powered analytics capabilities.
- **Features**: Sentiment analysis, brand monitoring, performance reports.

- **Utilities**: Measuring the impact of social media marketing campaigns, competitor analysis.
- **Industries**: Marketing, PR, Sales.

6. Tableau

- **Description: Data** analytics platform that allows users to visualize data and share information.
- **Features**: Predictive analytics, data integration, interactive visualization.
- **Utilities**: Data-driven decision making, trend identification.
- **Sectors**: Finance, health, retail, marketing.

7. Zoho CRM

- **Description**: Customer relationship management software that includes AI functionalities.
- **Features**: Sales automation, predictive analytics, chatbots.
- **Utilities**: Improved customer relationship management, sales optimization.
- **Industries**: Sales, marketing, customer service.

8. Amazon Web Services (AWS) AI

- **Description**: A suite of artificial intelligence and machine learning services available in the Amazon cloud.
- **Functions**: Image analysis, natural language processing, speech recognition.
- **Utilities**: Application development, business process automation.
- **Sectors**: Retail, finance, technology, health.

9. SAP Leonardo

- **Description**: SAP's digital innovation platform that integrates AI, IoT, and data analytics.
- **Functions**: Machine learning, predictive analytics, process automation.
- **Utilities**: Improved operational efficiency, customization of services.
- **Sectors**: Manufacturing, finance, retail, logistics.

10. HubSpot

- **Description**: Inbound marketing and sales platform that uses AI to improve the customer experience.
- **Features**: Chatbots, data analytics, marketing automation.
- **Utilities**: Improved customer acquisition and retention, optimization of marketing campaigns.

- **Industries**: Marketing, sales, customer service.

11. Pandas

- **Description**: Python library for data analysis that allows for effective data manipulation and analysis.
- **Functions**: Structured data management, statistical analysis, data visualization.
- **Utilities**: Data preparation for AI projects, trend analysis.
- **Sectors**: Finance, health, research, marketing.

12. Alteryx

- **Description**: Data analysis tool that allows users to prepare, blend, and analyze data.
- **Functions**: Data integration, predictive analytics, data modeling.
- **Utilities**: Data-driven decision-making, optimization of analysis processes.
- **Sectors**: Marketing, finance, health, retail.

13. Keras

- **Description**: Open-source deep learning library that enables the creation and training of AI models.
- **Functions**: Implementation of neural networks, rapid modeling.

- **Utilities**: Development of custom AI applications, research in machine learning.
- **Sectors**: Technology, health, finance.

14. TensorFlow

- **Description**: Open-source framework developed by Google for machine learning and artificial intelligence.
- **Functions**: Construction and training of machine learning and deep learning models.
- **Utilities**: Research and development of advanced AI applications.
- **Sectors**: Technology, healthcare, automotive.

15. Donors

- **Description**: Automated artificial intelligence platform that facilitates the construction of machine learning models.
- **Functions**: Automation of the modeling process, predictive analysis, visualization of results.
- **Utilities**: Agile development of AI models, optimization of business decisions.
- **Sectors**: Finance, healthcare, retail, manufacturing.

16. Qualtrics

- **Description: Experience** management platform that uses AI to analyze customer feedback.
- **Functions**: Sentiment analysis, market research, predictive analysis.
- **Utilities**: Improved customer experience, data-driven decision-making.
- **Sectors**: Marketing, human resources, customer service.

17. Freshdesk

- **Description**: Customer service software that uses AI to optimize incident management.
- **Features**: Chatbots, ticket analysis, task automation.
- **Utilities**: Improved customer service efficiency, quick response to problems.
- **Industries**: Customer Service, Technical Support.

18. Airtable

- **Description**: Database management tool that combines spreadsheets with database capabilities.
- **Features**: Workflow automation, integration with other AI tools.
- **Utilities**: Project management, task tracking.
- **Sectors**: Marketing, product development, human resources.

19. ChatGPT (OpenAI)

- **Description**: A language model developed by OpenAI that generates text in a conversational manner.
- **Features**: Autoresponders, content generation, customer support.
- **Utilities**: Improved customer interaction, content creation, response automation.
- **Industries**: Marketing, sales, customer service.

20. Lattice

- **Description**: Performance management and talent development platform that uses AI to improve human resource management.
- **Functions**: Performance evaluation, continuous feedback, analysis of work environment.
- **Utilities**: Improved talent development, employee performance optimization.
- **Sectors**: Human resources, talent management, training.

This list of tools provides a solid foundation for organizations to begin exploring and implementing artificial intelligence in their operations. The key to a successful implementation lies in selecting the right tools that align with the company's strategic objectives and the specific needs of your industry.

www.ingramcontent.com/pod-product-compliance
Lightning Source LLC
Chambersburg PA
CBHW071459220526
45472CB00003B/855